American Self-Taught

American Self-Taught

Paintings and Drawings by Outsider Artists

Frank Maresca · Roger Ricco

with Lyle Rexer

With a Foreword by Lanford Wilson

ALFRED A. KNOPF   NEW YORK   1993

This Is a Borzoi Book Published by Alfred A. Knopf, Inc.
Copyright © 1993 by Frank Maresca / Roger Ricco
All rights reserved under International and Pan-American Copyright
Conventions. Published in the United States by Alfred A. Knopf, Inc.,
New York, and simultaneously in Canada by Random House of
Canada Limited, Toronto. Distributed by
Random House, Inc., New York.

Library of Congress Cataloging-in-Publication Data
Maresca, Frank.
American self-taught/Frank Maresca, Roger Ricco with Lyle Rexer;
with a foreword by Lanford Wilson.—1st ed.
p.   cm.
ISBN 0-394-58212-8
1. Primitivism in art—United States.   2. Art, American.
3. Art, Modern—20th century—United States.
I. Ricco, Roger.   II. Rexer, Lyle.   III. Title.
N6512.5.P7M37   1993
759.13'09'048—dc20   93-267   CIP

Manufactured in Hong Kong

First Edition

For William L. Hawkins

Through his art he always sought to reveal the joy and love he had for all that came into his life. He did not fail. In seeing his art we know the gift of a happy and generous man—a teacher and friend. We are truly indebted to William L. Hawkins, a man who loved painting.

Acknowledgments

Our heartfelt thanks are owed to many, but especially to Phil Patton, who carefully attended to and refined the artists' biographical sketches, and to our editor, Vicky Wilson, whose patience, insight, and skill of craft enabled us to communicate our love of this art. Our special appreciation goes to the publisher's staff, particularly Ellen McNeilly and Iris Weinstein, as well as Marion Maneker and Antoinette White, without whose talents this project would not have been possible. At the center of our efforts has been our own staff, Susan Fingerle, Liza Greenwald, Linda Safran, Maggie Galton, and Manu Lawrence. Their enthusiasm and dedication sustained us.

Our thanks go especially to Lyle Rexer, whose literary contribution translated our thoughts and gave them life.

Finally, of the most significant importance are the photographs of Charles Bechtold. We are greatly appreciative of his most skillful talents.

Foreword

There's an old saw that asks, "Can man live without art?" There's no question that the world can be very beautiful. A shadow lying across the lawn (or the whatever), a chance juxtaposition of colors or textures can be as deeply satisfying as a painting (or a whatever). The violence and brutality of life create sufficient catharses. We don't need Cassandra to tell us we are family.

A critic (I can't tell them apart) once said that some march on Washington was the greatest play he had ever seen. There, finally, was real theater, real art. No. That was real life. I have no doubt it was an enormously uplifting experience for those involved (or distressing, depending on your side of the fence). But it wasn't theater and it wasn't a play and it wasn't art. Art is a phony, manufactured thing that creates a response in our life. It can be something that looks, or doesn't, very much like life. In the 1960s I spent some wonderful moments and got my feet dirty attending a number of happenings, being led through God knows what variety of mazes and group gropes, mental and palpable, but they didn't purport to be life. Art can take any form. It can be anything. It can be frivolous and silly or imposing and portentous; it can be remote, aloof, or disinterested, enigmatic or didactic; it can just be. It can teach and encourage; I suppose it could discourage. It can be so strange and silent even its maker or The Maker can't tell you what it is. Art can please, soothe, or assault. Richard Serra's Tilted Arc, which cut in half the public square people were used to crossing at lunch hour, was placed where it was for precisely the effect it had. Inconvenienced people who had professed their irritation were protesting what was probably the most profound artistic experience of their lives. Art doesn't have to go down like Southern Comfort. It can be very alarming if come upon unprepared.

Best to get rid of a few more truisms while we're about them: Art has nothing to do with community morality, and it has no truck with taste. It has no obligation and no responsibility. It doesn't even have to be true. Holbein's portrait of Anne of Cleves is a very slippery business. *Richard II,* historically at least, is a tissue of Tudor flattery.

Can we live without art then? I suppose I can imagine a rude upbringing (as with Romulus and Remus, or Tarzan) where one would never encounter art and still be the perfectly healthy individual we're all so concerned that everybody be. Where one might spend every waking moment embroiled in the tangibles of being, the hand-to-mouth syndrome, and would have no time or occasion for aesthetic considerations. Even a civilized soul might be able to get away for a while, to a cabin in Maine or the vicinity of Walden Pond, someplace where he can get through the week without accidentally witnessing art in spite of himself. But in our ordinary existence, not at the stretch of extremity (slavery, war, being fostered by wolves), we spend very little time experiencing . . . *life.* And whether we can live without art or not, I firmly believe that we cannot live without *making* art.

With the least wandering from the task at hand, our mind drifts into myth and fiction.

There is, however, a catch. All this drifting and musing is something the ordinary person keeps very close to his chest. There's a part of ourselves that we tell nobody. A woman I know spends a fortune lying to her psychiatrist. But this wandering is the stuff art is made from. Art is a risky business; it can be very embarrassing when it's good.

Confession number one: There are all kinds and varieties of artists—artists who sing, who act, who build buildings, take photographs, sculpt, write poetry or novels or plays; artists who make music or three-dimensional objects or paint. In all these media there is the artist who is working on a strictly cerebral plane, with no emotive intentions. I believe them when they say that their art is objective, but try as I might, to the extent that my mind understands and admires these equations, they alter my body temperature. I respond to this strictly cerebral work emotionally. Call it a blind spot.

There is an oddness in some people (probably the misalignment of some gene or other, and early in the next century it will be corrected, as what won't be) that inclines them to draw. Their hand, given a pencil or stick—doodles. We monitor our children quite closely, saying they are the hope of the world (they are, manifestly, but we rarely believe that), and young persons of at least moderate means who are found to have an overdose of this drawing gene have been for a while now, say since the Greeks, sent off to be with fellows of their bent, learn the jargon of their ilk, and be instructed in their craft quietly, out of everybody's way. They are not necessarily going to be our artists—only the most ordinary or traditional sort of talent is recognized as artistic, and all the wrong people are praised. But they learn to draw with all conceivable media, practice gesture, contour, chiaroscuro, the tricks of representing perspective, the theories and god-knows-what of color and principles of composition. They smudge and shade and blend, crosshatch and whatnot. With side trips into print-making paraphernalia that would confound the laity they advance through the monochrome media into pastels to watercolor to tempera to acrylic and triumphantly, as if surviving some mortal rite—to oils! (Or, lately, not to oils: Acrylic is a little glaucous, but who's to notice? And oil dries too slowly for a happening generation.) They learn how everyone has done everything from the cave painters to underpainters to whatever is going down tomorrow, often imitating these techniques. I don't actually know of a class in cave painting, but it wouldn't surprise me. They are instructed in the roots and rationalizations of the prevalent concepts, theories, practices, prejudices, and fashions and are graduated with: Go now into the world and be Thyself.

There is no reason why an artist shouldn't be armed with all the technique and theory the great schools offer. But this is a system that can keep the country in teachers, dealers, historians, and greeting-card illustrators. To survive such an ordeal with any kind of vision a student would have to be a genius, have a genius for a teacher, or flat-out slip through the cracks. To survive, the student would have to be—well, an artist. Technique can be taught, art can't.

Artists are born. They're born in all the varying circumstances of society. They are privileged or not, supported by their family or not, trained or not, and they move to a place where artists are accepted or they don't. Many live the life we all recognize from fiction as the Artist's Life. More power to them. They forge their way, push, demand, yell, create—you need a lot of strong positive verbs for these people.

Then there are artists who live to be seventy before they discover who they are. You hear the story repeatedly: I always wanted to be an artist, but I had to go to work, I had to drop out of school in the fifth grade, I married when I was young and started a business, raised a family. There are those who panic at the thought of what it is that's inside them. We are not necessarily given pluck and talent in equal measure. (I have a bagful of examples of timid artists, which we can omit.) But we don't often think about the courage it takes to be someone whom the community distrusts. I don't know how to say this without coming out and just saying it, but there are communities that don't much like artists. Artists make ugly, disturbing things. They make fun of tragic situations. They take jokes seriously, or religion seriously. Or lightly. They don't have a community vision. They can't be trusted. We make laws to protect ourselves from them. Maybe that's why some artists become so extravagant and exhibitionistic. They finally just say: Oh, to hell with you guys, here I am, like it or throw rocks.

Tangent: W. C. Rice is a deeply Christian man who has made an environment on a country route near Prattville, Alabama. Driving down the road you are suddenly in a valley with steep hills on either side that are covered with, buried in, thousands of white and red crosses and signs. They are everywhere. Giant crosses are outlined with smaller ones that bristle out all around them. Signs admonish Repent Now!, Died From Sex Used The Wrong Way, and the astonishing No No No Water In Hell. It's an amazing sight, as is the pickup Rice drives, with portraits of Jesus on the doors, slogans written on the sides, and a ten-foot cross, four feet wide, that springs up from its bed. If we know anything about the sort of man who drives such a vehicle, we know he isn't diffident. Rice told me it was three days after he erected the cross on the bed of his pickup before he found the nerve to drive it into Prattville.

We are familiar with the Struggling, Never-Appreciated-in-His-Time, Nothing-Could-Stop-Him-Not-Even-Madness-Until-He-Stopped-Himself myth. We know the Slightly-Effete, Salon-Full-of-Cognoscenti-Fawning-While-He-Paints myth.

Well, there are a couple more. There's the group of retired people, or residents of a nursing home, being given their first class in painting, with the teacher walking around looking at all their work, suddenly stopping at some seventy-year-old man's, or woman's, canvas and saying "Holy God, look at that!" And there's the seventy- or eighty-year-old woman, or man, who picks up a piece of roofing tin, paints something on it, props it up in the yard, paints another just to pretty up the place, and everyone driving by says, "Oh, my lord, look at that eyesore," until someone with a more discerning eye suddenly screeches to a halt on the highway because he's seen something nobody has ever seen before.

Mary Tillman Smith, on a highway outside Hazelhurst, Mississippi, uses plywood and found objects to make flat, bold portraits of herself and neighbors. She chops figures with a hatchet from used roofing tin, leaving sharp, dangerous edges and points, then paints the figures with wide graphic swipes of a brush: huge stick figures with quirky personalities, painted in poster bright or melting pastel enamels, with fewer strokes than any artist I know.

Smith is a spirit—she seems closer to the elements than any person I've met. On a warm day she held my hand tightly—I thought only my mother was that strong—saying, "It's so nice of you to come see me. I, oh—" and the rest of the sentence was lost in her amazement with the strength of the late fall sun, until finally she said, "On such a day!" I asked if she was still working. I didn't know if she heard me. Her eyes were closed, her face turned to the sun for a long time. Without opening them she finally said, "Oh, yes, I'm still working."

Smith had a mild stroke a few years ago. I had been told it would be difficult to understand what she said. It wasn't. She is somewhat self-conscious about her ability to make herself understood but she shouldn't be. While she was ill a dealer backed his truck up to her yard and (for a price, in cash, that would now buy one good-sized piece) carted everything off to a warehouse where it still lies. Her yard is immaculately well kept now and (surprise) she likes it that way. I was disappointed not to see the outdoor gallery that almost amounted to an environment, but that was just romantic nonsense. She works inside now, feeling more like "any other artists"; sometimes painting on material that is supplied by friends and "customers," sometimes on tin or plywood she locates herself. The power and originality of her work have not diminished a whit. Some prefer the weathered look of the pieces from her yard, or the rough surfaces of the found material she worked on when she first began to paint, just as they might prefer the found objects in Louise Nevelson's early work to the specially milled material she used later. To my mind's eye the two artists are a solid tie for the strongest woman American art has yet produced—early work or late.

After talking to near-saints like Mary T. Smith, Freddie Brice, and the wonderful Annie Lucas, it's a splash of cold water in the face, or cold reality, to come back to the streets of industrial Bessemer, Alabama, and Thornton Dial. He's never said outright that the tiger in his paintings is African-American Man (or a self-portrait) striding through the jungle in his adventures with the white man, characterized as a monkey, often on the tiger's back. But the monkey is boss in many of the paintings, and Dial will tell you that "Everybody likes to see the monkey climb." Of another painting he says, "Yeah, the tiger's getting pretty sick of having the monkey all the time staring up his ass." And, "This painting is of a man lying with his mistress. While the man is asleep that dog comes out of the mistress's side and eats the man's wife."

You will read that self-taught art is a phenomenon of the Industrial Revolution. I'm not so sure. Granted that the most alarming consequence of automation and such is that we have stopped using our hands to make things. Airplanes (believe it or not) are largely handmade, but cars are not. Except in quaint grant-supported enclaves, we don't throw pots or weave. The Taos Indians wrap themselves in pink-and-white striped flannel blankets from Montgomery Ward to dance their prayers. We no longer make our own shoes or most of our clothes, furniture is down to simple assembly, and who remembers American supremacy in anything except arms. But I think it's easier to believe that self-taught art has always been with us; that its recognition is a phenomenon of Expressionism. With the Expressionists we became interested in the subjective response of an artist. Since the Renaissance or thereabouts everything in art had been technique. Anything that wasn't technically up to snuff was discarded as unworthy. There are glimpses of these artists in early scrimshaw, Delft pottery, etched glass, face jugs, diaries, Byzantine mosaics, and illuminated manuscripts. Maybe we just found them late.

In any case, it is clear that the life experiences of many of these artists parallel those of our writers so closely that it shouldn't be surprising that their work is better related to American literature than to American art: Sam Doyle making icons of his island's history, Hawkins's farmboy amazement and delight in the buildings of Columbus, Esteves and Klumpp and Speller with their unabashed sexual fantasies. What a stunning draftsman Speller is, and what a shocker. His outrageous women, garterbelted or naked, in frankly sexual postures, and his drawing of the human sex organs—his absolute delight in them—make you realize how chaste and uninvestigative much of our art has been. For all our nudes, the body has barely been touched.

Confession number two: In the end, in these days of urban irony and deep cynicism, with so many artists painting with tongue in cheek, it was a deep relief for me to come across a group of painters who believed in something and laid it down uncensored. I realize that this work, as lightly as it can possibly be presented, will come crashing down on the heads of a lot of people who thought they knew what art was. I thought I knew, was pretty cocky about it in fact, and it slapped me (as mother would say) into next Sunday. It's a mystery why it has been so little known for so long. When writers for the trade journals and papers have found time to witness this work, they have received it well. More and more these artists are being represented in our museums. Many painters, always ahead of everyone, have known this work, have been deeply influenced by it, as is obvious, and have collected it for years. Actually, just now it's rather hot. God save us from the oblivion of fashion—the last thing anyone wants is for self-taught art to become the flavor.

As you have probably gathered by now, I'm a fanatic. Still, being very levelheaded, I know this book will introduce many new artists that will become very important to many new people.

I'm happy to help you make their acquaintance.

Lanford Wilson

American Self-Taught

American Self-Taught Art and the Recovery of a World

In his most famous story, "Tlön, Uqbar, Orbis Tertius," Jorge Luis Borges proposes a world within the one we know, yet hidden and invisible, a vast imaginative effort of a legion of creative people operating by secret agreement down through time. This world is complete in all its details, from its alternative cosmology and science to its legends and heroes. Evidence of it can be found in libraries and unexamined repositories of culture. Once discovered, this world exerts an irresistible fascination.

This book testifies to the existence of such a world—a broad, heterogeneous body of work by American visual artists, with its own energies, coherences, visions, and complex relations to artistic tradition and experience. Until relatively recently, this world—created by self-taught artists—was largely invisible. Our first book, *American Primitive,* was an attempt to bring to view its sculpture, assemblages, and other three-dimensional constructions and to show how many of these seemingly unprecedented works had deep roots in anonymous American "folk" and craft traditions. This volume brings together paintings, drawings, and other two-dimensional works by nearly a hundred self-taught artists. Few of the artists will be well known even to an artistically experienced public, and some will be new even to those who know the field.

It has been twenty years since Roger Cardinal's *Outsider Art,* echoing Dubuffet, made its brief but uncompromising statement for the importance of the more extreme forms of self-taught art, and nearly fifty years since the pioneering art dealer Sidney Janis attempted the first comprehensive, not to say definitive, view of self-taught art in *They Taught Themselves.* Janis himself helped stage the 1939 exhibition at the Museum of Modern Art titled "Contemporary Unknown American Painters," which followed by a year "Masters of Popular Painting." With these events, the museum culture first acknowledged in a broad way what Braque, Picasso, and many other modernists already knew—that the art of untrained individuals cannot be separated by quality, impact, or formal beauty from mainstream art. Yet the difference between the artists Janis selected (only four of whom are represented here) and the current group points up how dramatically the notions of what art is and who can make it have changed even since the revolution of Modernism.

In general, the works Janis chose for his book have the explicit or recognizable styles and ambitions of earlier academic or serious art, especially European art. The work is clearly "finished," and most of the artists appear aware that they are artists, performing a distinct and traditional function. Published after the Great Depression and World War II, the book is primarily a celebration of the European immigrant, the talented but "raw" Sunday painter, the common individual who has the ability to be "just as good" as his world-renowned contemporaries in their studios in Paris and New York. Henri Rousseau is, of course, the prototype. Only four artists are black. Criminals, the so-called mentally ill, and the socially marginal are, for the most part, excluded.

Much has changed. The work of the four holdovers from Janis—Horace Pippin, John Kane, Emile Branchard, and Morris Hirshfield (Victor Gatto was an honorable mention)—is by now well recognized and has withstood the test of time. Only a few others in this book refer stylistically to the earlier work. More than half of the artists in *American Self-Taught* are black or Hispanic. Over the last decade, art historians and museums, on the one hand, and prescient dealers, collectors, and artists, on the other, have widened the definition and appreciation of self-taught art. Often moved by what was immediately around them, they have helped legitimize many of the field's more marginal practitioners and begun, sometimes without intending it, to cut the works loose from comforting labels like "outsider art."

Paradoxically, however, developments in serious, or high, art have cleared the widest space for recognition of the world of self-taught art. We can do no more than sketch these developments, but increasingly it appears that the art of the twentieth century cannot be understood independently of self-taught art.

In a sense, the space began to be cleared when Gauguin, in rebellion against middle-class taste but more because his own work was at a dead end, forsook "painterly" values for a rebirth of the primitive in Tahiti. Romantic painters and writers such as Baudelaire had already launched an all-out attack on the Academy and its aesthetic norms. In their polemics they even used ancient art, especially Mexican and Egyptian, to establish a precedent for themselves. Moreover, as the critic John Berger points out in reference to the English prison artist Michael Quanne,

> Every style in art cherishes certain experiences and excludes others. When somebody tries to introduce into painting a life experience which the current style or traditional styles exclude, he is always dubbed by the professionals *crude, clumsy, grotesque, naive, primitive.* (It happened to, amongst others, Courbet, Van Gogh, Käthe Kollwitz, and Rembrandt.)

Artists such as Matisse, Picasso, Miró, Kandinsky, Chagall, and Klee, who thrived after many of the battles had already been fought, retained within themselves an affinity for both the primitive and the childlike in art and allowed these impulses prominence. Artists since Cubism have consistently sought formal, political, and spiritual inspiration from tribal, primitive, or popular forms, from ritual masks to cartoons. Cubists, Dadaists, and Surrealists broke down one of the most stubborn barriers of taste, the one defining what materials are appropriate to a work of art. When Kurt Schwitters snatched train tickets and other mini-icons from the detritus of an ordinary day, he was engaged in precisely the same aesthetic process—looking, analyzing, responding, hoarding—as William Hawkins on the streets of his Columbus, Ohio, neighborhood. Yet perhaps the most important development in recovering the world of self-taught art has been the gradual erosion of the distinction between "high" art forms and "low," or popular, ones. That development has been ongoing since at least the late nine-teenth century and reached a sort of watershed with Pop Art. We can appreciate the apocalyptic cartoons of Henry Darger in part because of the unrelated, even opposed work of Roy Lichtenstein and Andy Warhol. The history of modern art is bound up by implication with self-taught or so-called naïve approaches because that history contains so many examples of artists attempting to unlearn their training and reauthenticate the means of expression.

Today, with the increasing popularity of self-taught art, the relationship between high and low is even more fertile. It may also be more important than at any time. Many trained artists are looking to the work of self-taught artists to rediscover the validity of images and spiritual themes.

The images in this book show the range of self-taught styles—their astound-ing diversity. The book is not, however, encyclopedic. It reflects, first, our taste and experience. These works have in common a swerving of the artist's sensibility away from the normal or conventional, even in the most sincere attempt to mimic the familiar. Realism is a set of learned conventions, which can contradict the way life is seen and felt. Self-taught images constantly remind us that art does not mir-ror some established reality but instead illuminates experience. Arising from no specific milieu but underlying all the works is the artist's drive to testify fully to his or her circumstances.

One sign of the urgency of this drive is the artists' use of disparate materi-als—Sam Doyle's and Mary T. Smith's pieces of tin, Martin Ramírez's paper bags, Simon Sparrow's shards of glass, Jimmy Lee Sudduth's "sweet mud." Joe Light was discovered painting on expressway underpasses and sidewalks; Sister Gertrude Morgan, Jon Serl, and many others have drawn on window shades. Howard Finster has used just about everything. The selection of these materials is only partly determined by availability and proximity. The artists' use of unortho-dox materials always represents an aesthetic decision, for when they have access to a broader range of media, their choices can be selective and highly specific. Bill Traylor disliked pastels and clean paper. Frank Jones used only the colors red and blue. It may be more accurate to call these choices spiritual, rather than aesthetic. God is reputed to have told the self-taught sculptor William Edmondson to carve limestone. For Jones, red represented fire, and blue, smoke. Not everything the world offers makes a claim on the imagination.

Ultimately, the most striking fact about these artists is that they seem to have so little in common stylistically. There is as great a distance between the work of Mary T. Smith and Drossos Skyllas as there is between that of Jackson Pollock and Botticelli. Perhaps more. Only when we are willing to look at these paintings as complex and intentional symbolic expressions can we recognize that self-taught art represents the range of human capability and awareness, not some narrow segment of it.

Recognition has been hindered, to a great degree, by the words used to define areas or aspects of self-taught art. Each of the most common terms has a limited value, and all serve ultimately to insure that the work remains separate, restricted, stereotyped, only partially visible. "Folk art" implies origins in a community-based tradition of craft and symbol that fits only a few of our examples. "Naïve" is contradicted by the quality and seriousness of too much of the work. "Isolate" is almost always false in some way. "Outsider," the most popular expression, continues to carry with it the stigmatic and often misleading or irrelevant associations of mental instability and social abnormality. Within recent French criticism, the term has become a political label. "Self-taught" is the only label that is neutral, not pejorative. Perhaps, like the term "fine art," it is too general to tell us anything. Yet it does hint at the independence and energy that pervade this work, and at a peculiarly American willingness to reinvent the wheel whenever a new kind of wheel seems called for.

It is no accident that many of these artists began creating late in life, after their working years were effectively over, in a century that has come to demand nothing more physically creative of its elderly than mere existence. Moreover, many self-taught artists—Freddie Brice, Ray Hamilton, and Eddie Arning come to mind—were "introduced" to art by other artists and art therapists. But their responses are based on fit and feel. Ballpoint pen but not crayon, plywood but not cardboard—the first instinctive decision predicates a thousand others. Unlike fine artists, however, these painters rarely call attention to the process of discovery and decision. They certainly don't make it the subject of their work. But they don't hide this process, either, and when we can trace the roots of their decisions, we come close to the mysterious core of artistic creation. We can see Bill Traylor draw himself into a corner, so to speak, and then magically leap out of it by shrinking a head or bending a back. Here we recall William Hawkins's explanation that the found objects he selected as the basis for his images were ones that "gave him a gift." We can experience the gift after the fact.

The supposed inability to make aesthetic and formal judgments is only one of the stereotypes shattered by the images in this book. Another, more pervasive one is that these artists are completely idiosyncratic, that they participate in *no* common traditions, and that the symbolic languages they develop are private, hermetic, and impenetrable. A host of exhibitions and studies over the last ten years has elucidated the roots of some of the iconography and craft traditions shared by black self-taught artists as different as Minnie Evans and Elijah Pierce. Studies of Howard Finster's work have pointed up the rhetorical organization of graphic approaches influenced by proselytizing Christianity and its emphasis on verbal and visual testimony. J. C. Huntington operates within a familiar Pennsylvania Dutch imagistic tradition. Martin Ramírez, Eddie Arning, Antonio Esteves, and Louis Monza owe a debt to Meso-American art. And when Andrea Badami and Drossos Skyllas create their very different madonnas, they do so aware of their antecedents in the Renaissance, though many times removed and attenuated through sentimentalizing Christianity.

What identifies these latter two artists as self-taught is their inability to understand that the tradition is moribund, superseded, in bad taste. For these artists, "tradition" is not the constraint of earlier forms and norms, but a free-floating repertoire of images, styles, attitudes, and genres, any of which can serve to channel and release creative impulses.

Beyond these explicit connections, we can discover a host of analogies with forms of ancient art, from prehistoric cave paintings to Egyptian art to the painted masks of Oceania. These analogies are not meant as an attempt to sanction self-taught work, which hardly needs special pleading, but to point up a recurring problem in the way we look at pictures. It is a problem that so-called primitive art raises constantly. We recognize that images can be archetypal. A picture of a tiger, or a man hanging alone on a cross, or a woman and man embracing, speak to us in ways that are in some sense outside of time and independent of the way they are rendered. Styles, on the other hand—the Gothic, the Baroque, Fauvism, Expressionism—are thought to be purely historical. They are the response of artists in a culture to past work and to broader social and economic currents. They coalesce and are themselves eventually transformed. Self-taught art suggests, instead, that there may be only a few fundamental ways of presenting experience, and that none of these is ever forgotten or truly lost.

The lives and works of these artists also call into question the degree of their presumed isolation. Certainly many have never known prosperity or received an education. To varying degrees, some of them are isolated from a social, if not psychological, mainstream—thrown back upon themselves with little support but their own inner resources. The prison, asylum, and hospital are common institutions in their biographies. Nonetheless, the more we examine individual lives, the harder it becomes to generalize even on the significance of extreme situations.

The range of images in *American Self-Taught* will, we hope, further encourage more serious attention to the narrative and symbolic dimension of the works. All these artists are representational on some level: they fashion images. This raises the possibility always of their saying one thing and meaning something else. In case after case, approaching these paintings as organized artifacts pays huge dividends. We can't help "reading" Louis Monza's *Nazi Hospital* (p. 154) as a political allegory. In a very different vein, both Frank Jones and Henry Ray Clark have at the center of their meticulously detailed performances a central metaphor of their incarceration—the clock. Both spent time in the same Texas prison. In his early work Gregory Van Maanen gives us a deflected, symbolist presentation of the spiritual impact of the Vietnam War.

There are profound differences of intention and approach between self-taught and academic art. In general, for self-taught artists the impulse to make art and to communicate is transmuted into images and never into strategies. This is another way of saying that these artists have no sense of *fashion* in art, or of commitments to style and imagery for some merely temporary and local purpose. Whatever they invest of themselves in their work they invest all the time.

This all-or-nothing openness is perhaps the defining feature of self-taught art and the reason why it can serve as a means of recovering the world for all of us. It is an openness before us, a willingness to show us everything seen, felt, and imagined without qualification or apology. More important, it is an openness before all aspects of experience, inner and outer, from the comic and celebratory to the deeply unsettling to the ordinary and usually ignored. These artists show us dreams, wishes, histories, and fears transmuted into vivid symbolic narratives. Their attentiveness both to the world and to their own inner lives is absolute, and its evidence lies in a thousand miraculous gestures, from Bill Traylor's transformation of simple shapes into a one-legged man (p. 246) to the uncanny light of Sanford Darling's *Lagoon* (p. 50).

The depth and coherence of the images tend to emerge after the initial surprise and unexpectedness have worn off. Because many of the artists in this collection are professing Christians or were raised in a religious milieu, their images often carry a transpersonal authority. That should prevent any viewer from taking the work of even such extreme visionaries as Sister Gertrude Morgan or J. B. Murry as mere idiosyncrasy. For many self-taught artists the world, after all, is but an imperfect copy of a higher one, and by telling us about themselves and their passage through it, they are also telling us about another, larger plan of creation. We look at these pictures—even the most desperately private ones—and we feel, above all, that we are not alone. In the two dimensions of an image, something miraculous occurs—people are joined to people, human beings to animals, men to women, calamity to celebration, the artist to his world, and to ours.

Roger Ricco
Frank Maresca
Lyle Rexer

American Self-Taught

Eddie Arning

(1898–)

Is creativity a product of confinement? Can walls be a channel for artistic energy rather than a barrier to expression? These are the questions that confront us in the work and lives of many of the artists in this volume, including Eddie Arning, who has been institutionalized for most of his adult life.

Arning grew up on his father's farm in Germania, near Kenney, Texas, about fifty miles northwest of Houston. Bouts of depression and anger eventually culminated in an attack against his strict Lutheran mother. His first hospitalization was relatively brief. The second, beginning in 1934 when he was diagnosed with so-called dementia praecox, lasted for thirty years.

Like many other self-taught artists, Arning was introduced to art by a member of the helping professions, in this case a teacher employed by the hospital. Arning's style springs directly from this first contact with art. In 1964 the teacher offered him wax crayons, paper, and coloring books, whose flat restricted forms shaped his visual sense. His ability to master more complex arrangements of figures, colors, and patterns grew rapidly, as did his repertoire of materials and images. The first images appear to have been autobiographical, but he later took inspiration from newspaper stories and magazine photos, advertisements and other popular material, as he began to work in oil pastels, with which Arning lends a soft, glowing, almost floating quality to shapes.

After release from the hospital, Arning spent the next decade in a nursing home, where he continued to work, turning his room into a studio, often producing a drawing a day, and gaining a significant local reputation. In 1973, however, he was asked to leave the nursing home because of his refusal to abide by its rules. After he went to live with his widowed sister, he ceased drawing altogether. "That's hard work," he remarked. A long-established creative and physical equilibrium had been disturbed, and Arning has never been able to recover it.

UNTITLED, 1964–66
Wax crayon on paper
19″ × 24″

UNTITLED, 1968–70
Craypas on paper
20″ × 26″

UNTITLED, 1969–70
Craypas on paper
22″ × 32″

UNTITLED, 1964–66
Craypas on paper
20″ × 25¾″

UNTITLED, 1970
Craypas on paper
20″ × 25¾″

MAE WEST AS LIBERTY, 1968–70
Craypas on paper
20″ × 26″

Andrea Badami

(1913–)

When Andrea Badami was five years old, his family decided to leave Omaha, Nebraska, where he was born, and return to Corleone, Sicily. This was the first of several transatlantic crossings that would lend Badami's art a singular cultural mix, part southern Italian, part midwestern American. Opportunities were so limited in Sicily that his father sent Badami back to the United States in 1929, but he had no better luck here. Badami returned to Sicily in 1931, married in 1939, and saw his first child born in 1940. Drafted into the Italian army, he was captured by the British in North Africa and spent the war as a prisoner of war in India and England.

After mustering out in 1946, Badami took the first available boat from Palermo to the United States and was able to bring his wife and daughter over in 1948. By then he had settled into a job in Omaha with the Union Pacific Railroad, which he would hold for thirty years.

This back-and-forth quality of his life is reflected in a style of painting whose overall symbolic thrust and arrangement of elements are European but whose subjects and use of pop images are distinctly American. Certainly his artistic inspiration was American: In 1960 in an Omaha art gallery he saw painting he regarded as "junk." Convinced he could do better, he began painting himself. His first work was done on the walls of his own house.

His work was discovered and exhibited by curator Tom Bartek of the Creighton University Museum in 1966, where his *Madonna Nursing the Baby Jesus* caused something of a stir. Badami often discussed his paintings and their obscure symbolic meanings in classes at the university.

Badami, however, is a perfectionist as well as an exegete, and in the 1970s he destroyed between forty and fifty of his pictures. He also painted over others that dissatisfied him with new works. Badami lives in Tucson with his wife and three of his four children, where his goal, he has said, is the creation of one perfect masterpiece.

BATHING MOTHER AND SON, 1970
Oil on canvas
32½″ × 48″

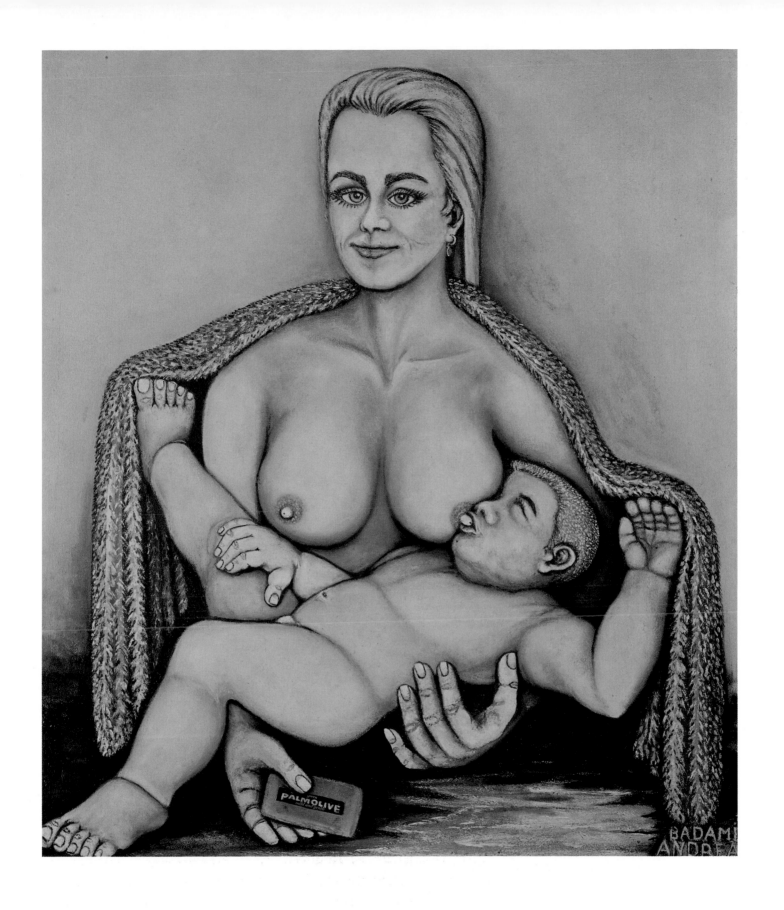

MOTHER NURSING CHILD, 1974
Oil on canvas
36″ × 31¼″

RESTING, 1984
Oil on canvas
40″ × 30¼″

Peter Attie ("Peter Charlie") Besharo

(1899–1960)

After Peter Besharo's death, the garage he had rented behind a local hardware store in Leechburg, Pennsylvania, where he had lived unassumingly for forty years, was found to contain sixty-nine paintings of visionary originality. Although he was something of a town character, his artistic efforts remained unknown to everyone around him during his lifetime, Besharo seems to have enforced a distance from people in the town, making many acquaintances but few friends. Yet to a few of those who knew him, Besharo hinted at the visions expressed in his paintings, almost as if he were preparing the world to understand what the garage held.

Besharo remains a mysterious figure, but recent research has substantially altered the biographical record and forced reinterpretation of his work. He was not born in Armenia, under the name of Peter Bochero, as originally thought, but in Syria, and probably came to the United States around 1912. Early on Besharo was a peddler, selling dry goods near Leechburg. Later he took up sign and house painting.

In his art Besharo revealed the complexity of his inner life, juxtaposing Arabic motifs with a variety of figures, from Native American warriors and angels to the crucifixion and creatures from outer space, as well as with such common occult symbols as the sacred eye. Though obscure at first viewing, these works are organized along the two axes of Besharo's spiritual life as a devout Catholic: the reality of suffering and the power associated with transcendence.

UNTITLED, ca. mid-1970s
Oil on canvas
34″ × 36″

UNTITLED (ALL SEEING EYE), ca. 1950s
Oil on canvas
38⅜″ × 53⅛″

NOMESOME, ca. 1950
Oil on paper
23″ × 29″

UNTITLED (WILL THIS PLANET BE RULED BY ANGELS' POWER), 1959
Oil on canvas
27½″ × 22½″

EVE WITH SPIRITS, 1950
Oil on paper
23″ × 29″

"Prophet" William J. Blackmon

(1921?–)

The philosopher Kierkegaard's famous joke about the man who, seeing a
FOR SALE sign in a laundry, rushes in only to find that it is the sign itself that
is for sale, perfectly describes the circumstances of Prophet Blackmon's "discovery." For years in the late 1970s and early 1980s, Blackmon had been battling
his landlord over the admonitory religious signs, with their allegorical images
and sermonizing rhetoric, that he displayed above his Revival Center and Shoe
Repair Shop in inner-city Milwaukee. No sooner would the landlord order them
removed than Blackmon would put them up again. One day in 1984 a passerby
offered to buy one—as art—and Blackmon discovered a way to communicate his
uncompromising moral message to a wider audience.

That message has developed over a lifetime of difficult experiences. Blackmon was born in Michigan and lived for a number of years there and in Ohio,
Illinois, and Wisconsin. He served in World War II and soon after took up street
preaching. His apparently accurate prediction of one friend's recovery from serious illness and of another's sudden acquisition of wealth earned him a reputation
for second sight and for healing powers. Blackmon's prophecies, as he embodies
them in image and text, often combine references to both biblical salvation and
extraterrestrial presences, whose triumphs are presented as the
consequence of mankind's sins—chief among them drunkenness, adultery, and
abandonment of the home. Blackmon and his art are fixtures in his neighborhood, where he has lived off and on since the 1970s, and when he isn't painting,
he works to encourage pride, self-respect, and hard work among his neighbors.

UNTITLED, 1987
Oil on wood
30″ × 20″

ESCAPE FROM HELL TO HEAVEN, 1986
Oil on wood
36″ × 36″

"Prophet" William J. Blackmon   / 23

Freddie Brice

(1920–)

Whether the subject be sacred or mundane, "painting gives me joy," says Freddie Brice.

Brice paints devils and animals, but he is just as likely to depict aspects of his immediate life—images and objects he collects and scenes from memory. He will often paint the same subject—his hat or his room on Manhattan's Upper West Side—repeatedly, varying his treatment, each time revealing a different aspect of the scene. Brice's joy in painting seems to overflow, for he sings and chuckles while he works, sometimes explaining his work in a steady banter filled with Gertrude Stein–like repetitions.

Brice was born in Charleston, South Carolina. His father left home when Brice was young, and he was raised for a time by his mother, who worked in a cotton mill. Brice came north to Harlem in 1929 and worked variously as a stoker, an elevator operator, a laundryman, and, most importantly, as a ship painter at the Brooklyn Navy Yard. These periods of employment were bracketed by longer periods of institutionalization—reform school, jails, and psychiatric facilities. It was through a psychiatric day program that Brice was first introduced to painting in the early 1980s.

Using enamel on boards sometimes as large as eight feet square, Brice works in the single-room-occupancy flat he has occupied for more than twenty years, or at the local community center.

HOLE IN THE HEAD, 1987
Oil on board
19½″ × 15½″

B29, 1988
Oil on canvas
30″ × 36″

UNTITLED, 1989
Enamel on found board
36½″ × 48″

BATHROOM, 1990
Acrylic, craypas, and varnish on wood
32″ × 48″

Freddie Brice | 27

David Butler

(1898–)

The visits of collectors and admirers that brought David Butler's brightly painted tin constructions and window shutters to a wide audience also led to the end of his production as an artist. Butler created around himself a world that both reflected him and protected him from that outside. After his work was shown in the Corcoran Gallery's 1982 "Black Folk Art in America" exhibition, Butler's shotgun shack outside of Patterson, Louisiana, was frequently visited by would-be buyers of his art.

As delightful as David Butler's individual assemblages and paintings can be (the director of the New Orleans Museum of Art, William Fagaly, who did the most to publicize his work, has called his art "a celebration"), his work was woven into the fabric of his life and was the expression of a particular place. Unfortunately, that place—Butler's remarkable shotgun shack—was dismantled in the mid-1980s after illness forced him to move in with his sister in 1983.

Butler, who is also a wide-ranging raconteur, insists that he has drawn most of his life, in spite of the fact that as the oldest of eight children born to a carpenter father and a missionary mother, he was largely responsible for raising his siblings. In his spare time he carved the scenes and animals he saw around him. His career in a sawmill, where he worked at a series of jobs from cutting

NATIVITY SCENE, 1982
Enamel on cut tin
27″ × 31″

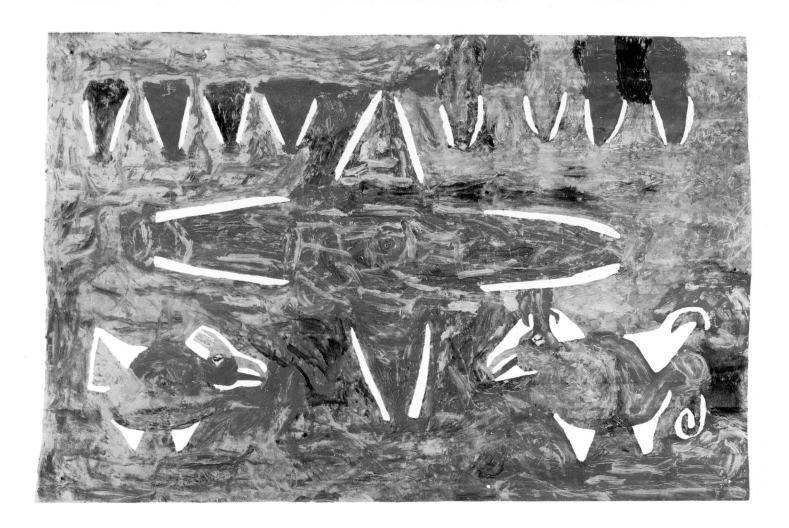

BLUE STAR, 1968
Enamel on cut tin
28″ × 42″

grass to working the dragline, came to an abrupt end in his late forties following an injury, and his career as an artist commenced.

He began to cut shapes from tin sheet using a hammer and chisel, then painted them with enamel and house paint and placed them around his house. While not entirely abandoning familiar scenes, over time Butler came to rely more and more on dreams and fantasy and introduced such images as sea monsters and lizards to his complicated windmill and whirligig assemblages. One of his favorite motifs is a four-pointed star that has antecedents in Haitian and African art. By covering the windows of his house with tin sheets perforated with precise patterns, Butler protected the interior from the intense Louisiana sunlight while at the same time creating complex patterns of light and shadow inside.

Butler was never at ease away from the environment his art created around him. Even his short travels in the area were made on a bicycle he decorated and painted. When the New Orleans Museum of Art mounted an exhibition of his work in 1976, the Good Hope Baptist Church raised money to take the entire congregation to the opening. Butler, characteristically, declined to go along. Now confined to a nursing home, he has done little work since leaving his home.

TWO LEAPING PORPOISES AND FISH, 1968
Enamel on cut tin
28″ × 42″

TWO RAMS AND PROPELLOR, 1968
Enamel on cut tin with plastic
28″ × 42″

FIRST NATIVITY, 1968
Enamel on tin with applied materials
28″ × 42″

Edward Patrick Byrne

(1877–1974)

UNTITLED, 1966–73
Enamel on cardboard
8″ × 14″

Set under vivid, monochromatic skies, the flat, geometric buildings rendered by Edward Byrne in the last eight years of his life achieve an almost Mondrian-like purity. Although most of them are based on photographs in newspaper real-estate advertisements rather than on first-hand observation, the paintings never-theless manage to evoke an almost palpable sense of the bold light of the Missouri plains where he spent most of his life. Byrne painted until his death at the age of ninety-seven at the Prairie View Rest Home in Lewistown, Missouri.

Byrne was born on a farm near Medina, in central Missouri. Over the course of his life, he came to be regarded by both his family and his neighbors as a progressive if unorthodox farmer, and as eccentric and outspoken. He did not create art earlier in his life, but the farm offered him ample space to exercise his talents. He was a self-taught musician and decorator. When he painted his barns and outbuildings, he labeled each with its characteristic animal—chickens on the chicken coop, horses on the barn. When he decided to redecorate his living room, he painted the walls with alternating stripes of color. He also built and painted birdhouses—hundreds of them. Their simple outlines and straight geometries seem to have found their way into Byrne's later paintings, which also included images of farm scenes, horses, and friends.

UNTITLED, 1966–73
Enamel on cardboard
8″ × 14″

UNTITLED, 1966–73
Enamel on cardboard
8″ × 14″

Edward Patrick Byrne / 33

UNTITLED, 1966–73
Enamel on cardboard
8″ × 14″

Henry Ray Clark

(1936–)

In 1977, during his first prison term, Henry Ray Clark "picked up a piece of
paper and the pencil went crazy in my hand." Since that moment, his intermit-
tent career as an artist has been precisely concurrent with the periods of his
incarceration.

Born in the small Texas town of Bartlett, Clark was three years old when
his father moved the family to Houston's Third Ward, notorious for its gambling and narcotics. Clark made his own way on the street from age sixteen, two
years after dropping out of school with a sixth-grade education. There his primary preoccupation was, in his words, "the almighty buck." Clark supported
himself by gambling and earned the nickname The Magnificent Pretty Boy,
which appears in some of his paintings. He served thirteen months for his first
conviction, for attempted murder, during which period he produced some sixty
of his heavily patterned, symbolic images using ballpoint pen, felt marker, and
pencil. "I didn't know there was money in this," he has said.

Clark was convicted four years later of narcotics possession, released again
after thirteen months, and rearrested on the same charge in 1987. Convicted,
Clark drew a thirty-year sentence under Texas's habitual offender statute. He
was sent to Walls Prison in Huntsville, where the legendary folksinger Lead-
belly and another important self-taught artist, Frank Jones, had spent time.
Clark's work was discovered by his prison art teacher, who he hoped would
teach him how to draw realistic faces, and his work appeared in prison art
shows. Clark's unusually sanguine attitude toward life behind bars springs
partly from a Christian fatalism and partly from the clear focus art has provided
for his energies. "They can lock up my body," he has said, "but they can't lock
up my mind. As long as my mind can create something beautiful to look at, I
am a free man, and I will live forever in my art." Supporters managed to have
Clark's term reduced but he was rearrested while on parole in 1992.

UNTITLED, 1988
Marker and pen on paper
8½″ × 14″

THE MAGNIFICENT PRETTY BOY—SIDE A, 1988
Marker and pen on manila folder
10″ × 17″

WE WILL WIN THIS WORLD—SIDE B, 1988
Marker and pen on manila folder
10″ × 17″

Henry Darger

(1892–1973)

Not even Nathan Lerner, the closest thing to a friend Henry Darger had, knew that each day for forty years, after Darger returned to his tiny Chicago apartment from his work as a janitor, he gave himself over to a vast artistic effort to represent the conflict of good and evil. Only after Darger's death, when Lerner, the building's landlord, finally entered the room did he find, among the religious artifacts, the hundreds of pairs of shoes, the dozens of pairs of shattered eyeglasses, and piles of newspapers and phone books, Darger's testimony to the triumph of innocence, a 19,000-page illustrated saga, *The Story of the Vivian Girls in What Is Known as the Realms of the Unreal or the Glandelinian War Storm or the Glandico-Abbienian Wars as Caused by the Child Slave Rebellion.*

Henry Darger's apocalyptic cartoons are as hermetic and troubled as the life he led. Darger was born probably in Chicago in 1892, barely knew his mother before she died, and was raised by his father, a tailor. After his father became ill, Darger was sent to a Catholic mission and then to an asylum from which he repeatedly ran away. In 1915, he was first hired as a janitor (a job he would hold and lose at various Chicago hospitals for the next forty-eight years), and by 1920 Darger was at work on *Realms of the Unreal*. He often illustrated his epic of seven saintly prepubescent slave girls, victimized by cruel masters, with tracings he took from magazines, newspapers, and comic books. These he had photographed and enlarged to carefully calculated sizes. He shaded his scenes of battle and cruelty with delicate pastel watercolors, and to accommodate the grand scale of his elaborate vision, he worked on both sides of sheets of cheap paper that he glued together in lengths of up to twelve feet.

Darger remained a devout but deeply conflicted Catholic throughout his life, and it is possible to view the entire body of his work as a believer's inquisition of God's working. In addition to *Realms of the Unreal*, Darger also left a 2,600-page autobiography, *The History of My Life*, a large portion of which is occupied with the description of a tornado he once witnessed, and a weather journal, in which he rigorously compared weather predictions with outcomes—as if the sign of divine justice might be hidden in a high-pressure system. When Darger could no longer climb the stairs to his apartment, he asked to be driven to the Little Sisters of the Poor Home, where his father had died, and spent the last few months of his life there.

AT GENNIE RICHEE: AT CEDERNINE—SIDE B, ca. 1950
Mixed media on paper
18″ × 70″

THEY ARE ALSO CLEVERLY OUTWITTED—SIDE B, 1960
Carbon, pen, pencil, and watercolor on paper
24" × 108½"

AT CEDERNINE, 1960
Watercolor and pencil on paper
19″ × 36″

at Cedernine
after rushing deadly peril
her sisters rescue her

above: CLOUDS IN THE WEST, 1960
Watercolor and collage on paper
24″ × 108½″

below: AT GENNIE RICHIE, 1960
Mixed media on paper
19″ × 89″

UNTITLED—SIDE A, 1950
Watercolor and collage on paper
24″ × 95″

AT ADERNING—SIDE B, 1960
Graphite and watercolor on paper
19″ × 36″

Sanford Darling
(1894–1973)

When Sanford Darling died in Santa Barbara, California, in 1973, he was a legendary figure and his house a local landmark that had been visited by some 8,000 people. The "House of One Thousand Paintings," as he called it, was decorated inside and out with images of scenes from around the world painted on plywood, cardboard, and other surfaces. Some were famous places, like the Taj Mahal, and some not, but Darling had visited almost all of them himself and through his art made each of them both personal and exotic.

By the time he was forty, Darling had already been a Hollywood stunt man, a commercial fisherman, and a chiropractor. From ages forty to sixty-five, when he retired, he worked as an engineer for General Petroleum, in Santa Barbara. After the death of his wife, alone and bored by his retirement hobbies of fishing and golf, Darling began to travel in Europe and the Orient.

Shortly after his return home, he was inspired to turn the impressions gathered during his travels into art. The first image came to him while he was painting his house and the green semigloss enamel he was using suggested a grass hut he had seen in the Pacific. This one image turned into the work that would occupy the last few years of his life. Darling fitted his paintings to the interior and exterior spaces of his house: on the roof peak a harbor scene, on a screen door Mt. Fuji, and inside his refrigerator a pastoral scene. As his house gained renown, partly as the result of an article in *Time* magazine, Darling became a sort of tour guide to his own home—and his own imagination—providing detailed explanations of the origins of all his images to visitors. In spite of its fame in Santa Barbara, his house was sold after his death and Darling's art was separated from the location that he had made the most exotic of all.

BLACK WATER, ORANGE HUTS,
1960
Enamel on Masonite
18″ × 24″

LAGOON, 1960
Latex on composition board
49″ × 49″

William Dawson

(1901–1990)

It took William Dawson more than a decade of artistic activity to return to the form that originally sparked his creative interest—painting. The first YMCA-sponsored art classes he took after his retirement in the mid-1960s were lessons in painting and ceramics. But either the classes or the modes themselves were uncongenial, and Dawson turned to wood carving, which he mastered wholly on his own. In truth, however, Dawson never stopped painting, for in decorating his now well-known wood carvings, he carried out experiments with color and pattern. The faces of his carved figures display the same preoccupation with eyes and mouths as his two-dimensional work. Dawson began painting again in the late 1970s, and as this activity assumed equal importance with his wood carving, he produced his most powerful pictures.

Dawson's artistic career unfolded entirely in Chicago, where he moved from a farm near Madison, Alabama, in 1923, soon after marrying his wife, Osceola. For thirty-five years in Chicago, Dawson worked for a produce distributor and eventually became a manager. After he retired, the odd jobs he took could not hold his interest, and he began classes at the Y. Though Dawson often enjoined his audience not to take his work too seriously, by the end of his life it was highly regarded. Dawson was included in the Corcoran Gallery's "Black Folk Art in America" exhibition in 1982, and just before his death in 1990, the Chicago Public Library mounted a major exhibition of his work.

UNTITLED, 1987
Tempera on paper
14½″ × 16″

UNTITLED, 1986–87
Oil on paper
11½″ × 17¾″

Thornton Dial, Sr.

(1928–)

"Art ain't about paint. It ain't about canvas. It's about ideas. Too many people died without ever getting their mind out to the world. I have found how to get my ideas out and I won't stop. I got ten thousand left."

Since as far back as he can remember, Thornton Dial has always created things. As a self-taught artist who has had little education and no exposure to the formal art world, he developed a style that is truly his own.

Thornton Dial, Sr., was born in Alabama in 1928, and never knew his father. He and his two brothers were passed around from one relative to another, all women. For thirty years Thornton worked for the Pullman Standard Company, manufacturer of railroad cars. It is not surprising, then, that the favored medium of his early work, mostly patio furniture, was metal. By the early 1980s Dial had begun to explore a far wider range of materials including plywood, canvas, and in some of his assemblages, plastics. He recycled his pieces as he needed material, and buried many of them when the yard became too cluttered.

His work encompasses subjects ranging from the most intimate, personal experiences to the most expansive philosophical observations: "If my art don't rub off on somebody, it ain't art"; and "I make art that ain't speaking against nobody or for nobody neither."

The range and versatility of Thornton Dial's work take one completely by surprise. Dial's medium is predominantly oil and enamel on plywood, frequently on 4′ × 10′ panels. Most of his works are paintings with relief elements. The line between painting and sculpture fades as he assembles vividly colored freestanding works. He incorporates bits of found objects into his pieces in keeping with his quasi-mystical philosophy of "recycle."

EIGHT WOMEN'S HEADS WITH
EIGHT SNAKES, 1989
Enamel on plywood
48″ × 96″

MEN ON ALERT, ALL EYES ON IRAQ, 1990
Oil on canvas
72″ × 78″

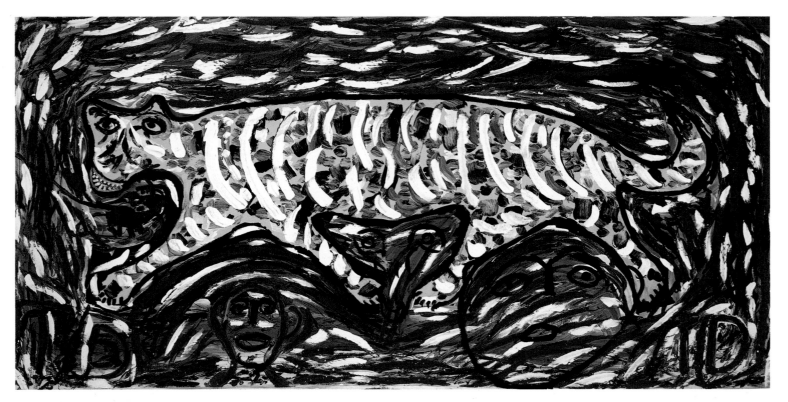

SCRAMBLING FOR LIFE, 1989
Enamel on canvas
48″ × 96″

SPIRIT OF THE GRAND CENTRAL STATION, 1990
Oil on canvas
60″ × 96″

Thornton Dial, Sr. / 55

JUNGLE PICTURE, 1989
Enamel on plywood
48″ × 96″

Sam Doyle

(1906–1985)

Well into this century, the Sea Islands on the coast of South Carolina remained an isolated enclave inhabited by the descendants of slaves. The residents spoke their own West African–inflected language, called Gullah, and carried on cultural traditions with strong African elements. Sam Doyle was born and spent his entire life on one of the islands, St. Helena, near a hamlet named Frogmore. He created a diverse and colorful gallery of local characters—real, like his cousin, the island's first black midwife, and imagined, like the ghost "Whooping Boy"
—scenes from island history, and legendary events, such as Abraham Lincoln's mythical visit to the island.

Doyle was one of nine children born to farming parents. His teachers at the island's Penn School, established by northern philanthropists, noticed his artistic abilities before he was a teenager, and one even invited him to go north to New York to study art. Instead, he was forced to go to work after ninth grade at a variety of jobs, first as a stock clerk, then for twenty years as a porter in a warehouse, and finally, from 1950 to 1967, in the laundry of the nearby Parris Island Marine Corps base. Doyle also acted as caretaker for the Chapel of Ease, a noted ruin in Frogmore.

In the mid-1940s Doyle's wife and their three children left him to move to New York, and Doyle began to paint. He used what was plentiful and accessible—roofing tin and enamel house paint. From the beginning, Doyle's work was like a public conversation, a form of storytelling, and he often hung his paintings outside his house for local residents and visitors to see and buy if they chose. One of the few times Doyle ever left the island was for the landmark Washington, D.C., exhibition "Black Folk Art in America." When he arrived, Doyle wanted only one thing—to return to St. Helena as quickly as he could.

ONK SAM, 1978–81
Enamel on found board
31½″ × 21″

JACKIE ROBINSON STEALING HOME, 1978–81
Enamel on tin
51″ × 36″

RAE (RAY CHARLES), 1981
Enamel on tin

GOOD TIME WOMAN, 1970–77
Enamel on tin
49″ × 37″

E. HOLMES, 1978–81
Enamel on sheet tin
56″ × 36″

Peter Paul Drgac

(1883–1976)

Born to immigrant Czech parents, Peter Drgac spent most of his life in and around the central Texas Czech community of Caldwell. He married a local woman in 1905, and together they owned and operated a grocery and bakery. A colorful and popular character in Caldwell, Drgac was known as Uncle Petc by friends and neighbors.

Around the time of his wife's death in 1962, Drgac's health began to deteriorate. Physically unable to continue his lifelong hobbies of carpentry and gardening, Drgac, at the age of eighty-five, began his career as a painter. During the next eight years (until his death in 1976), he produced hundreds of decorated objects and paintings. He began by decorating household items such as tables, chairs, disposable egg cartons, and light bulbs, using brightly colored enamel house paints and small paintbrushes. He quickly expanded into paintings that were done primarily on poster board covered with an enamel wash.

Drgac's style is reminiscent of much Eastern European and Czech folk art in its stylization, use of stenciling effects, bold primary colors, and decorative repetition of shapes. Drgac continued to experiment with different techniques, materials, subject matter, and colors over the years. He turned his small house into a gallery, virtually wallpapering the main rooms with his paintings, and welcomed visitors. "If you like the pictures, bring you friends," he would say.

UNTITLED, ca. early 1970s
Enamel on paper
22¼″ × 14½″

UNTITLED, 8/25/71
Enamel on paper
21″ × 13″

Victor Duena

(1888–1966)

LADY AND DOGS, 1966
Mixed media on paper
12″ × 16″

In the early 1960s, patrons of the Vesuvio Cafe in the North Beach area of San Francisco began to notice unusual paintings hanging on the walls. The striking images were simple in outline but with their wild-animal subjects, intricate patterns, and dense, jungle-derived palette of greens and browns, they suggested the exaggerations of myth. Their maker, Victor Duena, lived not far from the cafe in a cheap hotel, where he created hundreds of these works in little more than six years. Many of them were sold to patrons of the cafe.

Duena's life remains largely undocumented. Born in the Philippines, he may have come to the United States as a merchant seaman and settled on the West Coast. He worked at a series of menial jobs for a large part of his life, including janitor, houseboy, dishwasher, and jack-of-all-trades. He didn't begin to paint until he was nearly seventy, and it is not known what initially motivated him. Once he began, however, he developed quickly, and his later paintings display a sophisticated handling of space and perspective, especially on a large scale. Duena also became more self-conscious of his role as an artist. Once when the Museum of Modern Art borrowed a work from a New York show for a rental exhibition without asking him, he demanded it be returned.

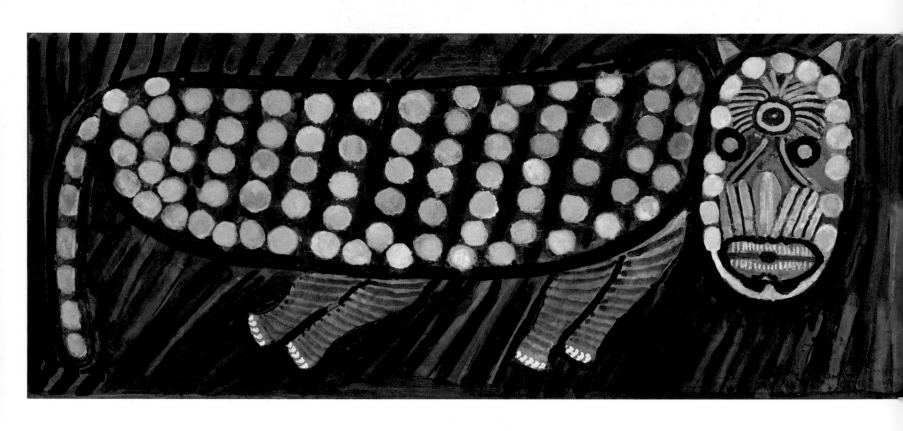

LARGE SPOTTED LEOPARD, 1966
Oil on board
13¼″ × 31″

Antonio Esteves

(1910–1983)

Although Antonio Esteves was only seven years old when he came to the United States from Rio de Janeiro, the painting he began almost sixty years later expresses deep affinities with a rich tradition of Brazilian self-taught art, as well as older forms of Central American religious art.

Esteves grew up in New York City. His mother died not long after the family arrived in the United States, his father was often away at sea as a ship's carpenter, and he was raised mostly by an extended family and friends.

He found a job as a building superintendent, married, and raised five children. He began to paint at age sixty-three after he was incapacitated by a boiler explosion in the Brooklyn building where he worked, as therapy during his recuperation.

After recovering, Esteves kept painting, using house paint on discarded boards. He opened an exotic pet store, but continued to work in a basement studio, taking his subjects from memory and dreams, which he would sketch upon waking and later used as a basis for his paintings. "You know," he once remarked, "as soon as I start painting, I forget my surroundings, I forget my aches and pains and everything else."

Both his enjoyment and his technical ability grew rapidly. He progressed from simple still lifes to large and ambitious compositions, such as his painting of Christ's crucifixion. Esteves lived across the street from the Brooklyn Museum, which he often visited, and the prize he won in a Museum-sponsored outdoor art fair in 1976 brought him to the attention of a curator. That recognition and the sale of several paintings made him realize that his work could be more than "therapy treatment," and he eventually came to regard his own work as the equal of Leonardo da Vinci's.

UNTITLED, 1977
Enamel on plywood
24″ × 35½″

UNTITLED, 1974
Enamel on board
21½″ × 29½″

Minnie Evans

(1892–1987)

Minnie Evans's ancestors were brought to the United States as slaves from Trinidad, and in her edenically lush, colorful crayon-drawn gardens, the island influences are palpable. Evans was born in a log cabin in Long Creek, North Carolina, and left school after the fifth grade to sell clams and oysters. In 1908 she moved with her family to Wrightsville Beach, near Wilmington, North Carolina, where she spent virtually the rest of her life (except for an uneventful trip in 1966 to New York City, which did not impress her). After 1918 she worked as a domestic. She also married and raised three sons. She began drawing in 1935 but did not begin working in earnest until sometime in the 1940s. In 1948 she took the job she would hold for twenty-eight years—as gatekeeper at Airlie Gardens, part of the Pembroke estate where she had worked as a domestic.

This tenure coincided with her most productive years as an artist. Sometimes inspired by biblical texts, but more often working from dreams and waking visions, Evans created a world that, though rich in detail, almost always carried the symmetrical, nonspecific contours of symbolic vision. Evans herself could not explain what the images meant. During these years she grew significantly as an artist and started using oils as well as crayon and graphite. Evans stopped working at Airlie Gardens in 1974 and moved to a nursing home in 1981, where she continued to draw until her death.

UNTITLED, 1946
Mixed media and collage on board
20″ × 24″

UNTITLED, 1945
Graphite and crayon on paper
12″ × 9″

UNTITLED, 1945–50
Oil on cardboard (back of book)
11½″ × 20½″

Howard Finster

(1916–)

Howard Finster's highly public art springs from his primary vocation as a preacher, a calling he assumed in 1932 at the age of sixteen, in rural Valley Head, Alabama, where he was born. After moving to Georgia with his wife in 1950, Finster supplemented his preaching by practicing other skills, including plumbing, bike and television repair, taxidermy, and carpentry. In 1976, Finster says, an angel appearing in a vision spoke to him, saying "Make sacred art." All his activities since then, from preaching to tinkering to appearing on television, have furthered that end.

Like other self-taught artists called to testify for God, Finster establishes no hierarchy of image and text and observes no boundaries among forms of communication. To date he has painted more than 12,000 pictures, philosophized on thousands of "thought cards," and created perhaps the most famous folk environment in the world, the two-and-a-half-acre Paradise Garden, outside his home in Pennville, Georgia. All of these he regards not as ends in themselves but as means for spreading the word of God.

Finster has become one of best-known self-taught artists of his time, as much for his colorful personality as for his art. He appeared several times with Johnny Carson on *The Tonight Show,* had two works exhibited at the 1984 Venice Biennale, and designed album covers for the rock groups R.E.M. and Talking Heads. Almost overlooked in the spectacle of his success as a painter and as the creator of his garden, with its array of found objects and its thirty-five-foot tower, is the technical facility and enormous range of his work, which can be comforting, ecstatic, futuristic, or hectoringly apocalyptic. In Finster's art, universes real and imaginary become text for a sermon, angels meet flying saucers, and Elvis and Henry Ford share space with Jesus and creatures from the Book of Revelations. In recent years, sensing he has little time left to spread the word of the Lord, Finster has organized a family assembly line, employing some of his fifteen grandchildren to stencil, pattern, and paint grounds for works to increase his production.

HISTORY OF PLANT FARM MUSEUM—IT TOOK ME ABOUT SEVEN YEARS TO CLEAR OUT THIS JUNGLE KILLING OVER ONE HUNDRED SNAKES, AND CUTTING THOUSANDS OF TREES, BUSHES, VINES. AND THORNS. FILLING DITCHE. LEVELING CLEANING OUT GARBAGE THROUGHOUT, LABOR ALL BY HAND TOOLS, STANDING ON MUD PALETS RAKING OUT WATER WAYS FOR THREE SPRING BRANCHES. IT WAS SAID BY MRS. C.L. LOWERY THAT THIS PLACE ONCE WAS A LAKE WHERE MEN HUNTED DUCKS FROM SMALL ROWE BOATS, MR. C.L. LOWERY FORMER OWNER OF THIS LAND DUG INTO A CLAY POT OF INDIAN ARROW HEADS. IF HE FOUND OTHER THINGS ITS. UNKNOWN, SINCE THAT TIME I FOUND ONE SMALL PIECE OF YELLOW GOLD SHINING FROM THE MUD WHERE I WAS DIGGING. NOT TOO FAR FROM THE CLAY POT MR. LOWERY WAS A MUSIC TEACHER WROTE THE WORDS TO THE SONG LIFES EVENING SUN ALLSO STUDIED AND WORKED ON PREPITUAL MACHINE. 40 YEARS, I NOW HAVE REMAINS OF HIS MACHINE, MANY YEARS AGO I KNOW GOD SPOKE TO MY SOUL THAT THERE WAS SOMETHING FOR ME IN PENNVILLE AFTER. 40 YEARS PREACHING THE GOSPEL WITH OUT CHARGE, I THEN FELT LED TO BUILD A PARA- DISE GARDEN IN WHICH I WILL OPEN PRINT THE HOLY BIBLE VERSE. BY VERSE. THROUGHOUT. PLEASE RESPECT FOR CHRIST SAKE. W.H.F.

HISTORY OF THE PLANT FARM, 1982
Enamel on plywood
46½" × 55"

WEIGHT OF THE WORLD, 1982
Enamel on plywood
18″ × 44⅜″

UNTITLED, August 1978
Oil on Masonite
34¾″ × 18″

THE STORY MAP #1234, 1976
Enamel on plywood
41½″ × 59½″

THE DEVIL'S VICE, 1978
Enamel on plywood
21" × 23"

DELTA PAINTING, 1983
Enamel on plywood
28⅝″ × 45⅛″

Victor Joseph Gatto

(1893–1965)

Like Ernest Hemingway, Victor Gatto practiced his art as a form of physical self-assertion: the keynote of his art and life was a pugnacity that brought him public attention but obscured the value of his work.

An ex-boxer, Gatto prided himself on marathon bouts of painting, which would last up to twenty-six hours. He was generous to strangers, suspicious of friends, and disdainful of anyone who painted from life or models. He once got in a fistfight at a gallery show. Told his work resembled that of Rousseau, of whom he had never heard, he made a trip to the Museum of Modern Art, where he came to the immediate conclusion that the long dead French artist was imitating him. He managed to alienate the Rockefeller family, who abruptly stopped buying his work. Art dealer Sidney Janis relegated him to no more than a mention in *They Taught Themselves* because Gatto denigrated most of Janis's favorite artists.

Gatto was born in Greenwich Village, an area of New York City known for its artist community, when it was still largely an Italian neighborhood. His mother died when he was four, and his father placed Gatto and his four brothers in an orphanage. He was later raised by a foster mother, to whom he remained devoted until her death. At twenty he became a professional boxer, and a few years later was sent to prison for a robbery he said he didn't commit. At forty-five, the sometime steamfitter discovered he could make money selling art at the Greenwich Village sidewalk show, and he found his vocation.

Gatto built ordinary scenes into dramatic ones by rendering them in sharp, often fantastic detail, working with tiny brushes and impasto techniques. He became popular with collectors, critics, and journalists, but made little money from his work. He shuttled between a rented room in New York and Florida, where he grew fond of the dog tracks. In old age, he gradually lost much of his eyesight and with it his enthusiasm for painting. But he continued to draw until his death in Miami, at seventy-two.

FIRE ISLAND, 1948
Oil on canvas
23¼″ × 35¼″

NIGHTMARE, 1950
Oil on Masonite
16″ × 20″

Lee Godie

(1908–)

Living on the streets of Chicago since the 1960s, Lee Godie has become a well-known personage of the city. Proclaiming herself a French Impressionist, Godie for years sat daily on the steps of the Chicago Art Institute because it was a good place to attract an audience for her painting. She continued to sell her paintings there until a well-meaning curator pointed out to her that her work had little to do with French Impressionism. This comment sent her packing to a site on the North Side of the city where for over ten years she continued to paint.

Godie has painted many Chicago landmarks, but she prefers portraits and multiple portraits of idealized characters, including her favorite subject, Prince Charming, a generically handsome youth. She has also done her own version of the *Mona Lisa*.

For many years Godie had no contact with her family, but in 1989 an article about her in the *Wall Street Journal* caught the eye of Godie's daughter, Bernice Black. Black was able to track down the mother she had not seen for many years. But the reunion could hardly have fulfilled her expectations. Godie insisted she associated only with artists, so she demanded that her daughter take art lessons. These Godie promptly administered to her daughter, on the streets of Chicago.

In 1991 Bernice Black was appointed legal guardian for her mother, and Godie was moved to a nursing home not far from her daughter's home in Plano, Illinois, where she continues to paint.

PORTRAIT OF A MAN
(AFTER PICASSO)
Ink, oil, and postcard on canvas
25½″ × 19½″

THREE PORTRAITS, 1975
Ink and oil on sewn canvas
55½″ × 19½″

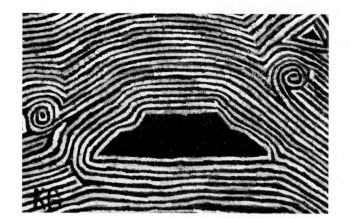

Ken Grimes

(1947–)

Is a man a closed system or is something added that possibly might come from outside the solar system?—Ken Grimes

For Ken Grimes that "something added" first manifested itself in the form of a science-fiction B-picture that he saw during his adolescence. The film, which depicted an ever-growing, brainlike, alien creature, was to be what Grimes considered his first real exposure to alien intelligence.

Grimes was born in New York City on July 16, 1947, a day that correlates—the artist is apt to point out—with other significant world events, including the first moon landing and the first A-bomb detonated in Los Alamos, New Mexico, in 1943. When he was still very young his family moved from Manhattan to Westchester County, to a suburb of Tampa, Florida, and back to New York City again before settling, when Grimes was six years old, in Cheshire, Connecticut, where he still resides.

Grimes's grandfather, a semiprofessional magician and inventor, left a long-lasting impression on the young Grimes.

The artist was first moved to deal with the paranormal, creatively, by an extraordinary circumstance. He discovered that the same time he was working at a public lottery in Cheshire, another Ken Grimes, sixty-two years old and living in Cheshire, England, won the largest soccer pool in history. This as well as many other coincidences have become part of what Ken refers to as the "Coincidence Board."

Since the Cheshire, England/Connecticut coincidence in 1971, Grimes's paintings have gone through a number of media and styles, but he has diligently maintained a theme of alien intervention, space signals, syncronicities, and government cover-ups. He paints only in black and white, which he maintains is the most direct way of showing the contrast between truth and deception. These bold white-on-black graphics have become more iconographs than pictures. Sometimes a written statement will take up most of the piece, as if to remind us of the painting's true purpose.

The sooner we start a pattern of global awareness and formulate a response to 'side affects,' the easier it will be to make the transition between a human-centered view and an alien perspective.—Ken Grimes

UNTITLED
(SAUCER WITH WAVES), n.d.
Acrylic on canvas
24″ × 30″

CROP CIRCLES, 1992
Acrylic on canvas
40″ × 30″

Dilmus Hall

(1900–1987)

When Dilmus Hall was traveling through Europe after serving as a stretcher bearer in World War I, he saw what European artists and craftsmen had produced over centuries, and he vowed he would carry back some of that artistic heritage and make it his own. This inspiration, joined with Hall's own craft experience and familiarity with southern Atlantic traditions of African-American imagery, yield a rich iconographic body of painting and sculpture. These works, displayed in and around Hall's house in Athens, Georgia, as well as the house itself, with its decoration of African religious symbols, have made the location a place of spiritual communication and instruction.

Hall was born in Oconee County, in the Piedmont area of Georgia, one of thirteen children in a sharecropping family. As a boy Hall learned how to use pine pitch bled from trees on the property as a modeling material. After World War I Hall was employed as bell captain at a hotel in Athens. He later worked for a concrete block fabricator, an experience that led him to create a number of concrete sculptures. As he said, "The more I would make them, the more I would understand about it." Hall began to gain local attention for the house and his work as early as the 1950s, but wider recognition did not come until the 1980s, when the work's originality began to be appreciated and its iconographic content better understood.

CHRIST ON THE CROSS, 1986–87
Graphite and colored pencil on paper
8½″ × 11½″

UNTITLED, 1983–86
Tempera on plywood
12″ × 21″

Ray Hamilton

(1919–)

The little that is known about Ray Hamilton comes from scattered revelations, written and verbal, offered by Hamilton himself. He was born most likely in Hampton, South Carolina. He served in the Navy during World War II and continued to address everyone he met with the military "sir" throughout his life, even appending the "sir" to his signature. After the war he moved to New York City and began working for the railroad. In the late 1970s, Hamilton was admitted to a state-run adult home in Brooklyn. He did not begin to draw until 1982, when a visiting artist introduced him to the red, green, and blue ballpoint pens that have become his trademark. Hamilton often works without models, drawing his animals from imagination and rural memories, but he is also apt to trace objects immediately at hand. These shapes he fills in with compulsively scored lines—Hamilton's trademark—until the shapes, shimmering and dynamic, take on a weight and life of their own.

WE ARE FISH, 1988
Pen and lead pencil on paper
24″ × 18″

UNTITLED, 1989
Ballpoint pen on paper
14″ × 18″

UNTITLED, 1988
Ballpoint pen on paper
17″ × 13¾″

TWO DOGS, 1989
Ink, pen, and watercolor on paper
15″ × 35″

William L. Hawkins

(1895–1990)

To accompany William Hawkins on his walks through the streets of his Columbus, Ohio, neighborhood was like following an experienced prospector in search of gold. Hawkins's selective eye seized images from newspapers, magazines, and advertisements for a suitcase archive he kept in his bedroom. He combined these images with his own recollections and impressions to create a vivid picture gallery of animals, American icons such as the Statue of Liberty, and historic events. And although Hawkins could barely read and write, he transformed words themselves, usually represented by his signature and birth date and often his place of birth, into powerful visual elements.

Born in rural Kentucky in 1895, Hawkins came north in 1916. His early years in Kentucky provided him with his knowledge and love of animals, an awareness that informs even his most fantastic dinosaur paintings. In Columbus, Hawkins held an assortment of unskilled jobs, drove a truck, and even ran a small brothel. He was married twice and claimed to have fathered some twenty children. Although Hawkins was drawing and selling his work as early as the 1930s, he did not begin painting in the style for which he is best known until the mid- to late 1970s. He worked almost without letup thereafter, in spite of illness and advancing age.

At first, Hawkins used inexpensive and readily available materials: semigloss and enamel paints in primary colors tossed out by a local hardware store, and a single blunt brush. Later, when he could afford it, he painted on Masonite, which he much preferred because it didn't "suck up the paint" like cardboard or plywood. Sometimes he dripped paint or let it flow across the surface as he tilted it so he could, as he put it, "watch the painting make itself." He often painted elaborate borders around his pictures and attached such materials as wood, gravel, newspaper photos, or found objects.

Hawkins suffered a stroke in 1989, from which he only partly recovered, and he died several months later. He once summed up his aspirations as an artist by remarking, "You have to do something wonderful, so people know who you are."

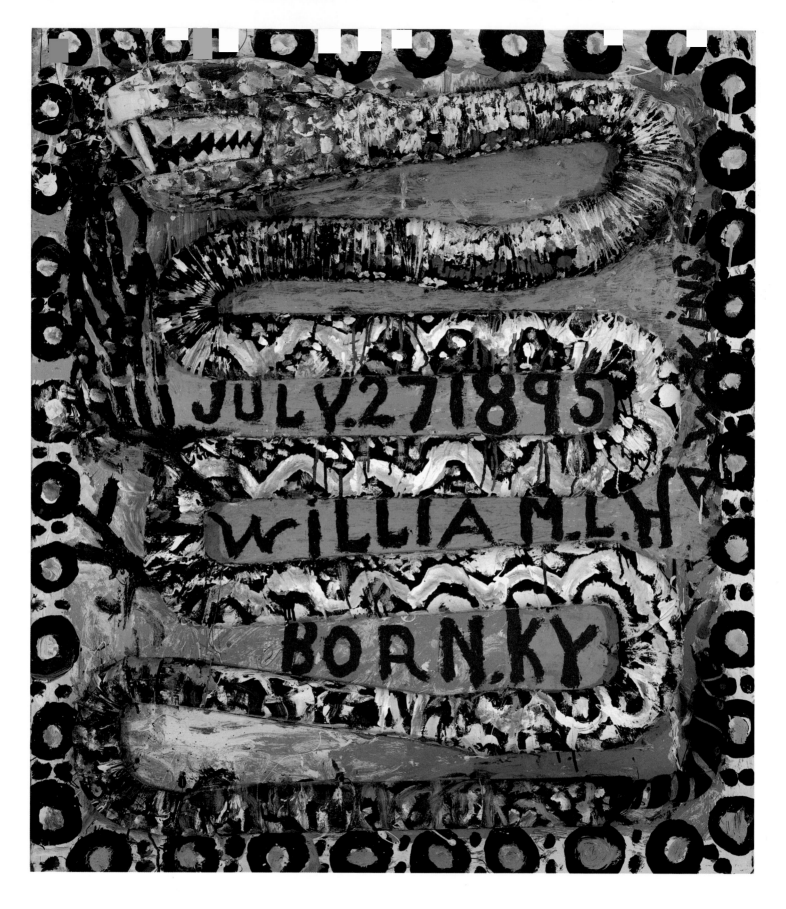

RATTLESNAKE #5, 1989
Enamel and mixed media on Masonite
56½″ × 48″

INDIAN HUNTING BUFFALO, 1983
Enamel and mixed media on Masonite
48″ × 62″

William L. Hawkins / 91

CONQUEST OF THE MOON, 1984
Enamel on Masonite
48″ × 56″

PRUDENTIAL, 1985
Enamel on Masonite
38" × 60"

William L. Hawkins / 93

HARRINGTON HOTEL, 1987
Enamel on Masonite
58″ × 46½″

REARING STUD HORSE, 1986
Enamel on Masonite
48″ × 56½″

Morris Hirshfield

(1872–1946)

Next to Grandma Moses and Horace Pippin, Morris Hirshfield is probably the best-known and most critically established American self-taught artist of the twentieth century. In 1943, after only six years of serious painting, Hirshfield was given a one-man show at the Museum of Modern Art, and forty years after his death, lavish editions of his work are still being issued by publishers.

Some of this continuing appeal springs from the biblical and European roots of Hirshfield's work. He was born in western Poland near the German border and, as he tells it, startled the village with his wood carving, first at age twelve and later when he fashioned an elaborate prayer stand for the village synagogue. At eighteen Hirshfield came to New York, where he worked in a coat factory. With his brother, he established his own firm to manufacture women's coats, then shifted to women's "boudoir" slippers. The brothers' E. Z. Walk Manufacturing Company became a tremendous success, at one time employing three hundred people and doing about a million dollars of business a year. Financial independence allowed Hirshfield to turn to painting when illness forced his retirement in 1937. In the nine years left to him, he produced seventy paintings.

Precise and painstaking, Hirshfield created an art where pattern is prominent—he was fond of woven and mother of pearl textures—and the curvilinear forms of his figures and animals portray a sense of contained energy that is at once sentimental and sensuous. Hirshfield's pictures appealed strongly to a generation of critics conditioned by Surrealism and Cubism. John Baur, a curator at the Brooklyn Museum, encouraged him to try his hand at painting nudes. Though modesty deterred him at first, the female figure became the subject of some of his finest later paintings. Hirshfield judged his self-taught contemporaries harshly, and often compared his own work unfavorably with that of far more conventional trained painters, now long since forgotten.

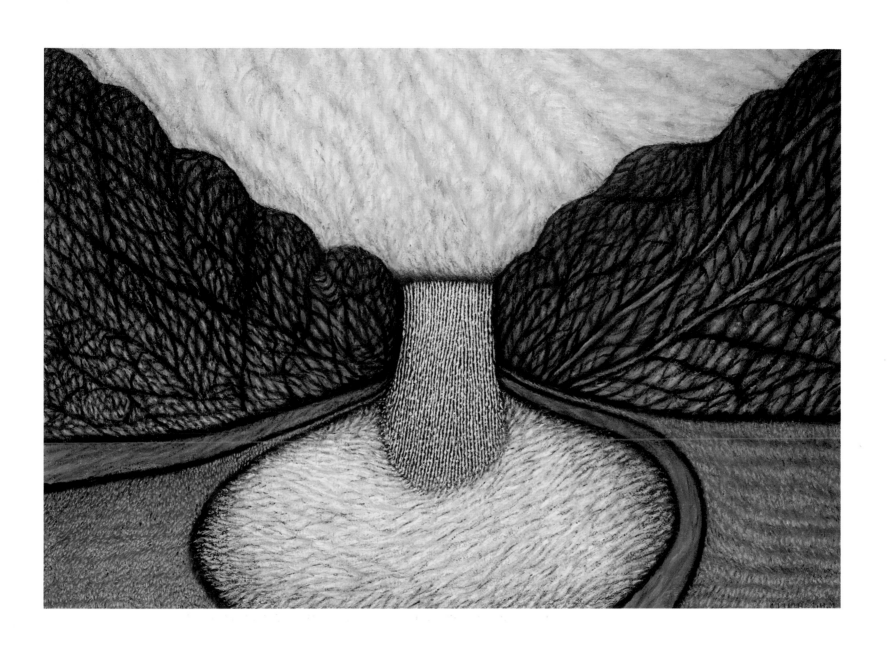

WATERFALLS, 1940
Oil on canvas
20″ × 28″

ZEBRA FAMILY, 1942
Oil on canvas
33½″ × 49½″

STAGE BEAUTIES, 1944
Oil on canvas
40″ × 48″

TAILOR-MADE GIRL, 1939
Oil on canvas
40" × 25"

Jessie Howard

(1885–1983)

Jessie Howard called himself "the man of many signs and wonders." Howard took to its furthest extreme the impulse toward visual religious testimony, common to many self-taught artists, by doing away with images altogether and using the world around him as a signboard. Beginning in the mid-1940s, Howard constructed an environment on his farm in Fulton, Missouri, that included his workshops and a chapel and incorporated hundreds of hand-lettered signs. Window shades, saws, lumber, even machinery carried Howard's religious messages. Done in ordinary house paint, the signs demonstrate Howard's instinctive understanding of form and surfaces, for each text is peculiarly adapted to the shape of its support. Unfortunately for the artist, many of his neighbors were not yet ready to receive his preaching, and Howard was constantly embattled and his property even occasionally vandalized by those who regarded him as a public nuisance.

Howard's obsession with language belies his lack of education. Born into a poor family in Shamrock, near Fulton, Howard attended school at best sporadically through the sixth grade. At the age of 18 he left home for several years to ride the rails. After returning to Shamrock, he married, bought the first of several farms, and raised a family of five children. It is unclear precisely what prompted Howard, supported by his wife's factory job, to begin constructing the environment he called "Sorehead Hill." In any case, Sorehead Hill allowed Howard to comment on events past and present, castigate his neighbors whenever they spoke or acted against him, and preach the Bible for nearly forty years.

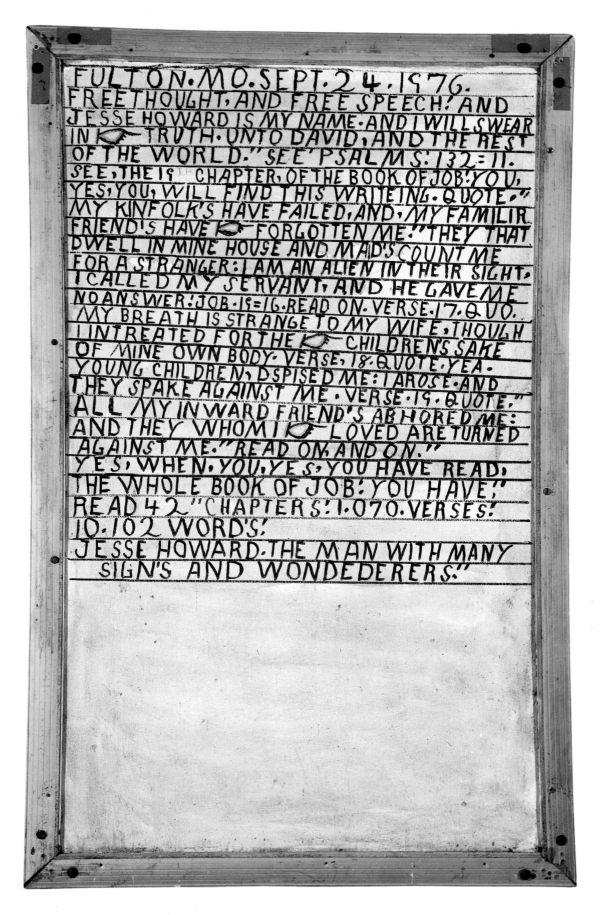

FULTON. MO. SEPT. 24. 1976.
FREE THOUGHT, AND FREE SPEECH! AND
JESSE HOWARD IS MY NAME. AND I WILL SWEAR
IN TRUTH. UNTO DAVID, AND THE REST
OF THE WORLD." SEE 'PSALMS: 132 = 11.
SEE, THE 19 CHAPTER, OF THE BOOK OF JOB YOU,
YES, YOU, WILL FIND THIS WRITEING. QUOTE."
MY KINFOLK'S HAVE FAILED, AND, MY FAMILIR.
FRIEND'S HAVE FORGOTTEN ME." THEY THAT
DWELL IN MINE HOUSE AND MAID'S COUNT ME
FOR A STRANGER: I AM AN ALIEN IN THEIR SIGHT.
I CALLED MY SERVANT, AND HE GAVE ME
NO ANSWER: JOB 19 = 16. READ ON. VERSE. 17. QUO.
MY BREATH IS STRANGE TO MY WIFE, THOUGH
I INTREATED FOR THE CHILDREN'S SAKE
OF MINE OWN BODY. VERSE. 18. QUOTE. YEA.
YOUNG CHILDREN, DSPISED ME: I AROSE. AND
THEY SPAKE AGAINST ME. VERSE. 19. QUOTE."
ALL MY INWARD FRIEND'S ABHORED ME:
AND THEY WHOM I LOVED ARE TURNED
AGAINST ME." READ ON, AND ON."
YES, WHEN. YOU, YES, YOU HAVE READ,
THE WHOLE BOOK OF JOB: YOU HAVE."
READ 42 "CHAPTERS: 1.070. VERSES:
10.102 WORD'S!
JESSE HOWARD. THE MAN WITH MANY
SIGN'S AND WONDEDERERS."

FREE THOUGHT AND FREE SPEECH, 1970
Oil on wood in aluminum frame
45¼" × 29¼"

Clementine Hunter

(1886?–1988)

Clementine Hunter lived her entire life of more than a century in the Cane River country of northwestern Louisiana. She was born in 1886 or 1887 on the Hidden Hill Plantation, which was said by locals to have inspired *Uncle Tom's Cabin.* Her mother was the daughter of a slave and her father was a Creole. When she was five, the family moved to nearby Cloutierville, where Hunter began school, from which she ran away after only ten days.

In her mid-teens Hunter and her family moved to the Melrose Plantation, outside of Natchitoches, Louisiana. Melrose was not only a working plantation but had become, under the direction of its owners at the time, James and Cammi Henry, a well-known and popular center for the arts and culture. There Hunter married, raised a family, and worked as a field hand for the next twenty years. In the 1920s she began working as a maid, and it was probably her talent for quilting and related "domestic arts" that attracted the attention of the plantation curator, François Mignon, who encouraged her with materials, including oil paints, and arranged for her first show in 1946 at Millspaugh's Drug Store in Natchitoches.

In the evenings, after the grueling day's work was done, Hunter recorded in bold, wide brushstrokes the plantation life around her, the ordinary events of picking cotton, washing, and churchgoing. Almost illiterate herself, she had a sign painted for her house that read CLEMENTINE HUNTER, ARTIST. 50 CENTS TO LOOK.

In 1955, when Northeastern Louisiana State University mounted a major show of her work, Hunter was able to visit it only after viewing hours: segregation laws still banned African-Americans from the gallery. Thirty-one years later the same university presented her with an honorary doctorate in fine arts. She was approximately one hundred years old.

THE HOSPITAL, 1980
Oil on paper
20" × 24"

TWO NUNS AND A PRIEST, 1942
Oil on paper
12″ × 13″

TWO-HEADED WOMAN, 1942
Oil on paper
12″ × 13″

BLIND LADY LEADING HER MOTHER, 1942
Oil on paper
12″ × 13″

J. C. Huntington

(ACTIVE CA. 1940–1950)

Although J. C. Huntington was active until the middle of this century, the style and subjects of his work are rooted in the last century. His paintings document the simpler rural order giving way to the industrial. Huntington, who was born in Sunbury, Pennsylvania, and sold his work in nearby Bloomsburg, painted in the static and flat geometric style so often associated with "folk" painting, particularly that of the Pennsylvania Dutch. Methodical and precise, Huntington used a compass to create the rounded shapes in his work and used his daughter as the model for the children in his paintings, whatever their ages.

Huntington began to paint after retiring from the railroad, for which he worked most of his life, and in his images of farm buildings and steam trains, animals and windmills, fields and machinery, traditional agricultural imagery is melded with newly arriving mechanical imagery.

Huntington's work was first brought to wider attention in the 1940s by Sterling Strauser, the Bloomsburg, artist who has been instrumental in fostering recognition for a number of important self-taught Pennsylvania painters, including Jack Savitsky (page 209) and Justin McCarthy (page 142).

UNTITLED, 1920–40
Watercolor on paper
20″ × 75″

UNTITLED, 1920–40
Watercolor on paper
20″ × 46½″

UNTITLED, 1920–40
Watercolor on paper
20″ × 46½″

UNTITLED, 1920–40
Watercolor on paper—double-sided
21½″ × 30″

Frank Jones

(1900–1969)

Stories and legends cluster around the life of Frank Jones like the drinking devils, gambling devils, and bird spirits of his drawings: He was born with a caul over his left eye and so it was said he could see spirits. His mother, a Creole, left him standing by a lamppost when he was three and never returned. He saw his first spirit presence at the age of nine. He witnessed a man struck by lightning for blasphemy. He had a premonitory vision, warning him of troubles to come.

The vision was accurate. He was born in the north Texas town of Clarksville and, after he was abandoned by his mother, was raised, alternately, by a neighbor and a relative, both stern fundamentalist Christians. As an adult, Jones did grueling plantation work, dishwashing, and other menial jobs until trouble found him. In 1935 he took in a seven-year-old girl, who he claimed was abandoned. He was raising her when her mother returned in 1941 and accused him of rape and kidnapping. He was convicted, and for the next two years, as part of his sentence, he wound the "haunted" clock in the Clarksville courthouse, an image that would figure prominently in his work. In 1949 he was implicated, under suspect testimony, in the murder of the woman who helped raise him, Della Gray. Paroled in 1958, he soon found himself back in Huntsville prison, this time for the rest of his life.

In 1961 he began drawing with stubs of red, blue, and green pencil the filigreed architectures he called "devil houses." He gradually populated these with various devils and spirits, which he called "haints." Sympathetic inmates and prison staff provided him with materials, and Jones created more than five hundred drawings in nine years. The fanciful, quiltlike patterns, which also suggest the Mexican-inspired imagery of homemade prison tattoos, possess a brooding sense of enclosure. In the mid-1960s, when Jones's parole request was denied, he began drawing a clock with its numbers running backward. Jones's gift for prophecy continued to the end: when he was sent to the prison hospital in 1969, suffering from cirrhosis, he correctly predicted he would not return.

DEVIL HOUSE, 1968
Colored pencil on paper
25″ × 38″

UNTITLED, 1964–68
Colored pencil on paper
22½″ × 24″

R. T. Jones

(DATES UNKNOWN)

SANTA'S BIRTHDAY PARTY,
1940–50
Enamel on plywood
30″ × 40″

Nothing is known about the artist who created this painting, which was meant to decorate the pediatric area of a hospital and was probably donated. The inscription on the back of the painting reads:

> If this picture brings just one smile to some sick child, I shall feel amply paid for the many hours spent upon it. To the nurse in charge: the various characters in this picture are taken from various fairy tales, including the following: Alice in Wonderland, Alice through the Looking Glass, Snow White, Red Riding Hood, the Reluctant Dragon, Aesop's Fables, Mother Goose, and a few others. In case some child wants to know why the flag of some nation is not shown, just explain that it is on the next wagon coming in at the lower left.

John Kane
(1860–1934)

In one of his most revealing pictures, *Touching Up,* John Kane offers a self-conscious image of himself dressed in workman's overalls putting the finishing touches on a painting in his apartment-studio, whose walls are lined with his own work. Throughout his life in America, this Scottish-born Irish immigrant actively sought training and recognition by the academic art establishment, but acceptance almost completely eluded him till the later part of his life. Twenty years after his death, however, he had become one of the most famous self-taught painters in American history.

Born in 1860 in West Calder, near Edinburgh, Scotland, Kane emigrated to the United States at age nineteen. He worked as an itinerant manual laborer, roaming through Alabama, Kentucky, Tennessee, and Pennsylvania until he lost his left leg in an accident in 1891 and settled for good in Pittsburgh.

Pittsburgh became Kane's muse, and he painted views of it repeatedly. He once remarked, "The city is my own. I have worked on all parts of it. . . . Why shouldn't I want to set them down when they are to some extent the children of my labors?" Kane's reputation rests primarily on these scenes, many of which include streets he helped pave or factories he helped build.

Kane married in 1897, but after the premature death of his third child he grew despondent and withdrawn, losing interest in almost everything except painting. He remained estranged from his family off and on for twenty-five years. At one point he attempted to enroll in art school, but lacking the money took a job painting railroad freight cars. During breaks, he would draw and paint his own images on the sides of the cars. At the end of his life he said that the best preparation for an artist was "to hire himself out to a good painting contractor."

Kane went on to work as a carpenter and a housepainter. In the 1920s, he enlarged and colored photographs and sold paintings door to door. One door he knocked on repeatedly was that of the Carnegie Institute, which finally accepted one of his paintings in 1927. After his first solo exhibition for the Junior League in 1931, he was revealed to have painted over photographs. He had no idea this practice was untoward. Thanks to a local reporter, Marie McSwigan of the Pittsburgh *Press,* who reported on his efforts to achieve recognition and later coauthored his autobiography, *Sky Hooks,* Kane began to enjoy a period of public and critical attention that would last till his death from tuberculosis in 1934.

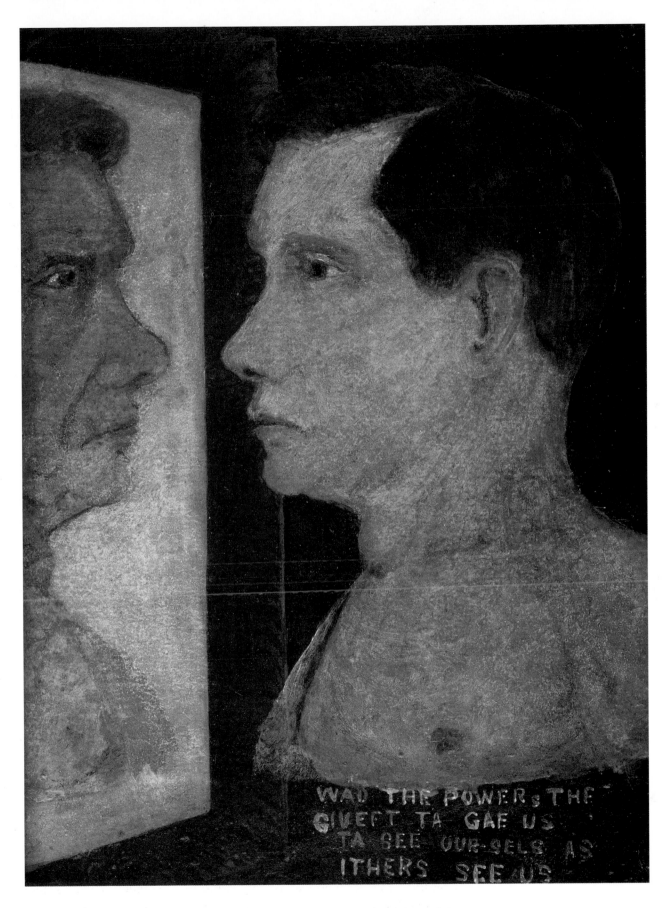

SEEN IN THE MIRROR, 1928
Oil on canvas
8½″ × 6¾″

THE GIRL I LEFT BEHIND, 1920
Oil on board
15 ⅜″ × 11 ⅛″

Charley Kinney

(1906–1991)

Across the creek from his family farm in a hollow near Vanceburg, Kentucky, Charley Kinney could see the cabin where he and his brother, Noah, were born. He lived his entire life with his brother and sister-in-law in this Appalachian setting, and his art is steeped in local lore and legends. These strains come together in the repeated figure of the "haint," as he called the demonlike spirit that plagues men. In pictures done on poster board with charcoal and tempera, Kinney often tells stories of his encounters with this spectral creature.

Charley and Noah Kinney have worked the land off and on for most of their lives, and both have been involved with art for decades. Charley cut hair, baked pies, and made split oak baskets to supplement his income. He also sculpted figures out of clay, including busts of famous people and figures of woodland animals that he sold to tourists. While Noah played the guitar, Charley accompanied him on the fiddle in performances punctuated with the telling of stories from the Bible and local folklore and the dances of puppets made from wood, scraps of fabric, and other cast-off items. Kinney began painting after the brothers gave up farming in the 1960s and let their place "go wild."

COATS, 1987
Acrylic and poster paint on board
22″ × 28″

UNTITLED, 1987
Acrylic and poster paint on board
22″ × 28″

Oscar William ("Pappy") Kitchens

(1901–1986)

Before O. W. Kitchens visited the North Carolina studio of his son-in-law, the painter Bill Dunlap, in the early 1970s, his art was limited to sketches he made on postcards sent to his family. Hanging around the studio, Kitchens began mixing acrylics and oils—to Dunlap's chagrin—and soon he was making his own paintings. Kitchens had retired from his construction business a few years earlier, and upon returning to Mississippi, he converted his garage into a studio and began to paint full-time. "Of course I made lots of messes, rubed [sic] out, painted over, got kicked around from one room to another, got paint all over everything . . ." In only a few years, he had earned recognition as a major self-taught artist, including selection of his work for the 1977 Corcoran Gallery Biennial.

Kitchens was born in Crystal Springs, Mississippi, to a Methodist farm family. His narrative visual art springs directly from the oral traditions of parable and storytelling he grew up with. His monumental sixty-panel work *The Saga of Red Eye, the Rooster,* painted between 1973 and 1976, presents a homespun Pilgrim's Progress in the form of a beast fable. Biblical renderings, as of the Seven Deadly Sins and such contemporary figures as Colonel Harlan Sanders, all figure in Kitchens's visual musings on how people ought to lead their lives.

Kitchens left home at the age of seventeen to ride the rails and "seek his fortune" in the West. By the 1940s, he had returned to Mississippi, taking a job farming. He later worked with a construction company of which he eventually became the head. Kitchens married later in life, to a woman many years his junior, and fathered one child. The untimely death of his wife, Ruby, from a heart attack in late 1985 was a severe blow to Kitchens, who had been suffering from Parkinson's disease since the late 1970s, and it most likely hastened his own decline and death, less than a year later.

MOTHER'S DAY, 1973
Oil on board
18½″ × 11¾″

TIME, 1973
Oil on canvas
35″ × 48″

GRANDMA WITH BOBBYE JEAN, 1975
Acrylic on board
17″ × 21″

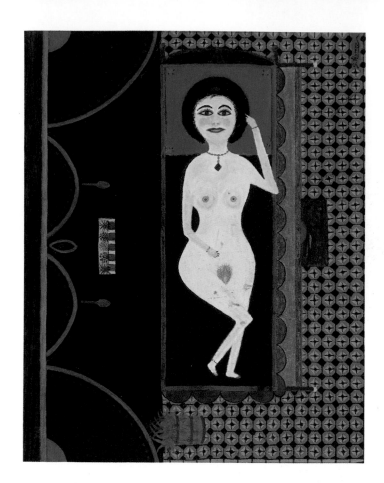

Gustav Klumpp

(1902–1980)

Gustav Klumpp's imaginary world is the kingdom of wish fulfillment—a world where marriages are celebrated naked and out-of-doors, where seminude women are always on display, and where, as Klumpp once wrote, there are always "gorgeous and colorful festivities going on."

Preoccupied as he was with the nude female body, Klumpp's expressed desire was not to titillate (although he makes at least one visual joke in his work about the artist's role as voyeur) but instead to add to the world's stock of beauty. Thus his nudist camps, beauty contests, and reclining nudes possess a willed innocence. One of Klumpp's most ambitious paintings, *The Wedding of King Glorious to Queen Gloria,* illustrates a children's story that Klumpp wrote in the late 1960s and attempted to sell to the Disney studio.

Born in the mountains of the Black Forest in Germany and trained as a linotype operator and compositor, Klumpp came to the United States in 1923. He worked in the printing trade for forty years. In 1966 Klumpp visited a senior citizens' center in the Red Hook section of Brooklyn and was encouraged to join an art group. He soon graduated from conventional historical subjects and landscapes to elaborate and colorful fantasies. What Klumpp once wrote about one of his works applies to them all: "Regardless the story is a beautiful fantasy or fictious [sic]. It is a story never to be forgotten." After barely more than five years of artistic activity, Klumpp ceased painting, saying he no longer felt well enough to continue.

UNTITLED, 1972
Oil on canvas
21¾″ × 27¾″

UNTITLED, 1970–72
Oil on board
15½″ × 19½″

Karol Kozlowski

(1885–1969)

In 1913 Karol Kozlowski arrived in the Greenpoint section of Brooklyn, New York, and became part of the arduous immigrant experience of industrial America. But Kozlowski created a refuge from that world—an unheated, unlit shed behind the house in which he lived, where he raised exotic birds and painted pictures.

Born in Kielce, Poland, Kozlowski was drafted into the Russian army in 1907 and served in Siberia until 1910. In 1913 he emigrated to the United States and soon moved in with a friend from his army days, Edward Gronet, with whose family he would live for the rest of his life. Kozlowski was illiterate in Polish and spoke virtually no English; the only jobs open to him were manual labor. In 1923 he began working for the Astoria Light, Heat and Power Company, removing the hot residue from the furnaces, a job he held for the next twenty-seven years.

Working evenings and weekends, Kozlowski created his earliest paintings as backdrops for the cages that housed his birds. Gradually, however, he came to devote time to the idyllic rural scenes and cheerful cityscapes for which he is known. Lack of space in the tiny, nine-by-nine-foot shed forced him to paint a section at a time on rolled-up canvases, which he usually did not stretch until after the painting was finished. In these works, with their smiling figures and local landmarks, Kozlowski expressed his idea of a world that was better, cleaner, less anonymous, and more hospitable than the one he knew.

In 1962 an elaborate painting of the plant where he worked brought Kozlowski to the attention of an art director for the power company, Abril Lamarque, who bought several of his canvases and introduced Kozlowski's work to curators at the Abby Aldrich Rockefeller Folk Art Center in Williamsburg, Virginia where it was shown in 1984.

JAPANS THOUSAND ISLAND MT. HUZI, 1960–65
Oil on canvas
51″ × 30″

Michael Lenk

(1891?–)

Flea markets and fairs have been essential commercial outlets for many self-taught artists and have led to many of them being discovered. No such discovery was more astonishing than that of Michael Lenk. Out of some seven hundred entries in the Arts and Crafts division of the 1965 Wisconsin State Fair Festival of Arts, the top prize was awarded to a vivid and detailed watercolor of the Garden of Eden, Lenk's *The Fifth Day of Creation.*

All that is known about the life of Michael Lenk, who repeated the subject in a larger oil painting of the same title, is contained in a brief biographical statement submitted to the judges along with the painting. Lenk was born in either 1890 or 1891, probably in Bohemia, from which he emigrated to the United States at the age of twenty-one. Lenk recalled that from the age of six he drew figures. "But I had no time to paint," he wrote, while practicing the trades of woodworking and carpentry in Milwaukee. Nevertheless, he maintained a strong interest in art, visited exhibitions, and even went so far as to enroll in the Allis-Chalmers Company's Sketch Club. After retirement, Lenk was able to devote himself to his art, but he would only paint during two seasons of the year, fall and winter. "I paint realistic," he wrote, "like things look." As if to prove it, Lenk numbered all the animals in his Garden of Eden and identified them on a separate sheet of paper. "I hope to live to paint many more," wrote Lenk at seventy-four, but only five paintings by this conscientious craftsman are known to exist.

GARDEN OF EDEN, 1957
Oil on canvas
30″ × 35″

Joe Light

(1934–)

Ever since Joe Light began to study the Old Testament while in prison, he has been engaged in a quest to redeem and beautify the world through art. Outside his home in Memphis, Tennessee, Light displays hand-lettered signs that admonish the viewer and comment on social issues. Inside, Light and members of his family have used painting both to decorate rooms and to establish a complex form of communication among themselves. Light's colorfully painted, cartoon-like flowers and other motifs have transformed objects as diverse as hubcaps and discarded television sets. Indeed, the more unaesthetic or decrepit the object, the more Light is committed to redeeming it: early on he painted highway bridges and sidewalks.

Born in Dyersburg, Tennessee, Light passed what he himself calls a delinquent adolescence during which he traveled throughout the South. In his twenties, he was twice sent to prison. The second time, he says, he converted to Judaism, whose beliefs he interprets in a highly personal way, calling himself a black American Jew.

After his release from prison, Light moved to Memphis and married his wife, Rosie Lee, with whom he had ten children. He sold bric-a-brac and secondhand items at flea markets and fairs. Around 1975 he began to paint his signs, to make driftwood sculptures, and finally in the mid-1980s to make paintings. Light once clarified the public side of his work, which has engendered some resentment in the surrounding neighborhood, when he remarked, "It's not about making people mad. It's about sharing what I know."

UNTITLED, 1988–89
Enamel on plywood
140″ × 48″

UNTITLED, 1977–78
Enamel on board
20″ × 26″

Ronald Lockett

(1965–)

A younger member of the extended Dial family, Ronald Lockett was, he says, always interested in art while in school. He was first stimulated to paint seriously by witnessing the creative activities of other members of the Dial family—and particularly by the extraordinary talent and influence of Thornton Dial, Sr.

Lockett's father and Thornton Dial, Sr., were both raised by the same relative, Sara Dial Lockett. Ronald Lockett was born in Bessemer, Alabama, in 1965, and after he graduated from high school he continued to live with Sara Lockett, but he frequently spent time at Thornton Dial's home, occasionally helping in the family business of manufacturing lawn furniture. It was there, at the Dial compound, that he was able to observe Dial senior's amazing resourcefulness at using found materials in his art: anything might be used in order to express an idea in a painting.

Though certainly influenced by Dial senior's free and bold use of diverse materials, Lockett's paintings are tied more explicitly to his own social and political concerns. His work ranges from allegories involving animals—for example, a skeletal deer or wolf trapped in a cage of real wire—to almost surreal, intensely psychological landscapes that might include houses in flames, torched by the Ku Klux Klan. In other paintings he has depicted his concerns regarding homelessness, the environment, the assassinations of John F. Kennedy and Martin Luther King, Jr., and even original sin in the Garden of Eden. Often his work will contain visual references to subjects he has painted previously, thus increasing the complexity of his painted message. Though Lockett works almost exclusively on raw or rough found materials, his painting technique remains both sophisticated and delicate.

TRAPS, 1988
Enamel, tin, and wire mesh on plywood
48″ × 49½″

REBIRTH, 1989
Enamel on plywood
30″ × 46″

DARKEST OF AFRICA, 1989
Mixed media on plywood
48″ × 62″

Annie Lykes Lucas

(1954–)

Raised with fourteen siblings in rural Autauga County, Alabama, Annie Lucas recalls watching her mother sew together flour sacks to make dresses for her and her sisters. Now, with six children of her own, she calls sewing "a regular necessity." It is also a distinctive element of her painting.

As early as the seventh grade, Lucas had the desire to make art, and she began painting after she married her husband, Charlie Lucas, in 1971. Her current work takes its inspiration from a vision she had in 1988, after she prayed for instruction on how better to render her artistic ideas. On the wall of her bedroom she saw the vivid and precise image of the biblical Jonah in the belly of the whale and made a painting of the image.

Since then Lucas has turned to the Bible as the source for her work. She uses acrylics on a variety of fabrics, including muslin, cotton, and canvas. She adds texture to many of her works by embroidering the painted surface, lending it a sense of three-dimensionality.

At the time of her artistic and spiritual epiphany, Lucas was working at the Autauga County Health Center, along with her husband. As her children have grown and outside interest in her work has increased, Lucas has been able to leave her job and devote more time to painting. That time is essential, for as she says, "It takes me so long to do even one."

SAMSON, 1989
Enamel and thread on cloth
17½″ × 23½″

UNTITLED (TWO ANGELS ON BLUE), 1989
Oil on fabric with stitching
19″ × 22″

JONAH AND THE WHALE, 1985–88
Oil on fabric with stitching
21″ × 28″

Dwight Mackintosh

(1906—)

Dwight Mackintosh's story really begins seventy-two years after his birth. Case records reveal very little about his life previous to his being institutionalized. He was born on May 19, 1906, and lived with his parents and brother in Hayward, California, until shortly after turning sixteen, when he was admitted into Sonoma State Hospital. The reasons for Mackintosh's initial institutionalization are no longer on record; however, a surviving court document indicates he had become "unmanageable at home."

After twenty-five years at Sonoma, on January 27, 1947, Mackintosh was transferred to DeWitt State Hospital in Auburn, California. There he spent another twenty-five years. On March 1, 1972, he was moved again, this time to Stockton State Hospital, where he spent his last six institutionalized years. Due to a growing trend in America of deinstitutionalizing the mentally ill and the mentally retarded, a decision was made to release Mackintosh. His brother, Earl, remembered Mackintosh's earlier interest in art and took him to The Creative Growth Art Center in Oakland, California.

In his new surroundings, Mackintosh was given the opportunity to draw and paint the visions he had formerly never expressed. Drawing became a compulsion for him, as he concentrated for hour after hour on his work, often falling asleep, dozing for a while, then waking to resume his work again. Art is our only insight into Mackintosh's world, for he is otherwise deeply withdrawn.

He draws mostly with felt-tip pens and sometimes uses watercolors and transparent inks, although color never takes precedence over line. Using sweeping, graphic lines, he approaches his work with abandon, yet his people, vehicles, and buildings are filled with an abundance of detail. Mackintosh's subject matter has remained virtually consistent throughout his time spent at The Creative Growth Center. People are his primary subject—mainly male figures who are shown alone or in groups, usually displaying erect penises of unusually large size. Most of these characters either have some sort of irregularity with their sex or they display some other anatomical deviation: more than ten fingers on one hand is not uncommon. His portraits are often depicted simultaneously frontally as well as in profile.

Seemingly unaware that he is "making art," Mackintosh produces his work with desperate intent, writing—in an unintelligible script—and creating images. When finished with a picture, however, he loses all interest, putting it aside and never referring to it again—another vision revealed and let go.

PIG FARMERS, 1988
Felt-tip pen and colored pencil on paper
22″ × 30″

ORANGE VEHICLE, 1982
Pencil and tempera on paper
23″ × 36″

THREE FIGURES, 1979
Tempera and ink on paper
22″ × 28″

MY MOTHER BAKING BREAD, 1988
Tempera, ink, and pastel on paper
22″ × 30″

Alexander Aramburo Maldonado

(1901–1989)

In 1961, when Alex Maldonado left the Western Can Company after more than thirty years on the production line, his sister had some ideas for his retirement. She made a point of showing him pictures of old men sitting idly on park benches; she also gave him a set of paints. Thus it was that Maldonado began vividly recreating scenes from his past on canvas and elaborating an arresting personal vision of fantastic cities on distant planets.

Born in Mazatlán, Mexico, Maldonado came north with his family to San Francisco during the revolution of 1910. By 1917 Maldonado was boxing professionally, under the name Frankie Baker. The ring would provide the subject of some of Maldonado's best-known images. He claimed to have shaken hands with "Gentleman Jim" Corbett and to have been chauffeured to his fights by former mayor of San Francisco "Sunny Jim" Rolph. After giving up boxing in 1922, Maldonado went to work at the Western Can Company.

Painting awakened something deep in Maldonado's being, and he threw himself into it completely. He worked all hours of the day and night in the basement of the Bernal Heights (San Francisco) house he shared with his sister. He decorated the entire surface of the basement, including the floor, as well as all his tools. Whether he was producing a visionary series of views from imaginary planets (perhaps inspired by seeing Halley's comet as a boy) or images of an underwater casino or observed street scenes, Maldonado described his method as "impressionism." Maldonado's sometimes somber palette began to lighten and diversify after he underwent a cataract operation in 1983. He described the result of his operation as miraculous, and called the works that followed "miracle pieces."

MALDONADO'S PLANET, 1987
Oil on canvas (double-sided)
12″ × 16″

MY HOUSE, 11/16/74
Oil on board
11¾″ × 16″

UNTITLED, 2/8/72
Oil on canvas
12″ × 16″

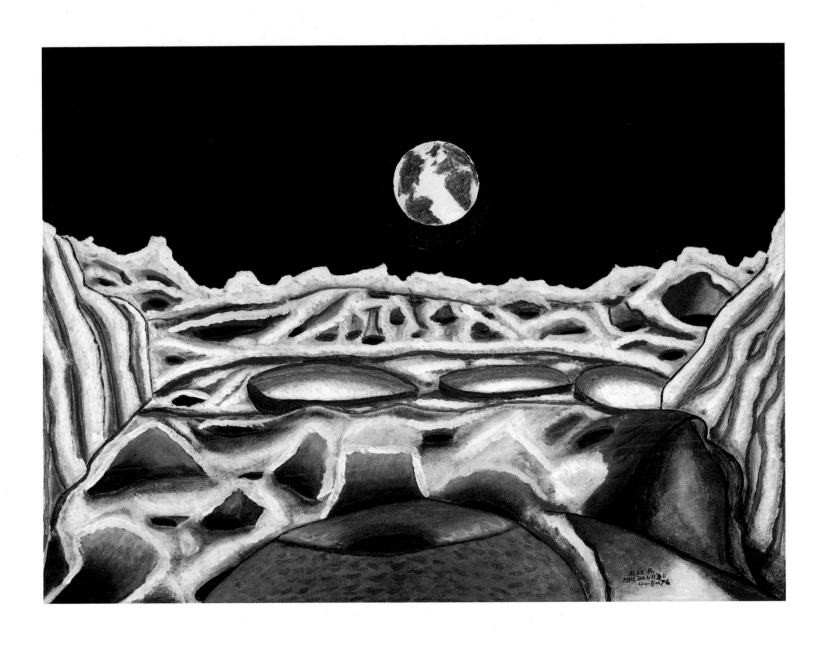

UNTITLED (VIEW OF EARTH FROM MOON), 1972–74
Oil on canvas
17½″ × 23½″

Alexander Aramburo Maldonado   /   139

Millicent Martin

(ACTIVE 1983–84)

Millicent Martin was active as an artist for only a brief period in 1983–84, while living at a public nursing facility in Brooklyn. There she was introduced to oil pastels by a visiting artist and began creating a vivid series of cats and people. Always a reluctant artist who needed considerable prompting to make a picture, she stopped making art altogether sometime before she moved to Yonkers in the late 1980s.

UNTITLED, 1986
Mixed media on paper
14″ × 10″

Justin McCarthy

(1892–1977)

UNTITLED, 1960
Oil on board
14½" × 37"

For Justin McCarthy, art seems to have served not only as a means of expression but also as a way of reforging and sustaining his links with the world. Born in Weatherly, Pennsylvania, in 1892, McCarthy was the elder and least favored of the two sons of a prominent father and a protective mother. As the result of stock speculation, McCarthy's father, a newspaper publisher, grew wealthy and set up as a gentleman farmer. He was also an avid amateur painter. This secure existence was turned upside down by a rapid succession of disasters. In 1907 John, Jr., the favored son, died, and in 1908 so did the father, leaving the family finances in disarray. Nevertheless, in 1911 McCarthy managed to enroll at the University of Pennsylvania Law School, while his mother took in summer boarders to make ends meet. But he failed his exams and suffered a nervous breakdown. From 1915 to 1920 he was confined in the Rittersville State Homeopathic Hospital for the Insane, where he began to make art.

McCarthy lived most of the rest of his life in the family mansion, including twenty years with his mother until she died in 1940. He made ends meet by selling fruits, vegetables, and liniment, and later by toting cement near Bethlehem. He also painted with a passion, filling rooms with oils, acrylics, and drawings. In its intense color and lively brushstrokes, McCarthy's work approaches most nearly the European Expressionists's. As well as working from life, McCarthy found his subjects in the mass media, painting actors he knew from films and entertainers and sports figures from television. He sold his work primarily at outdoor art fairs until 1960, when he began to receive wider recognition. In his later years until he moved to Tucson, Arizona, for his health, he was supported in his work by concerned collectors as well as by the citizens of Weatherly.

UNTITLED, 1955
Oil on plywood
11″ × 18″

UNTITLED, 1961
Enamel on Masonite
19½″ × 29½″

OREGON CLUB, 1961
Oil on Masonite
$23\frac{1}{2}'' \times 43''$

Justin McCarthy / 145

Kenny McKay

(1941–)

In Kenny McKay's drawings, and in the process of his making them, small rituals have enormous significance. McKay concludes every session of art-making by drawing a variation of the same image—a giant coffee cup, sometimes held by a hand. The image and the act of making it are linked for McKay, just as drinking coffee and drawing are both sustaining habits for him. McKay, who is of Armenian descent, was born in the New York area. At an early age he began to experience the learning impairments that led to his institutionalization.

For more than a dozen years, McKay has been creating watercolors of people, animals, and imaginary creatures, including dragons and unicorns. His work was ignored until he began to participate in an organized art-therapy program. He always begins with fluid contour drawing, sometimes focusing on a subject without looking at the line he is making. When this linework in finished, McKay then scrubs watercolor into the page. He will often overlay one subject on another. The watercolor then becomes a transparent medium through which the viewer peers at a complex interplay of line and form.

UNTITLED, 1987
Wax crayon on paper
12″ × 18″

EGG AND A SNAKE, 1987
Wax crayon and pencil on paper
13½″ × 10″

Laura Craig McNellis

(1957–)

Laura Craig McNellis was born on September 8, 1957, in Nashville, Tennessee, and was the youngest of four sisters. Her father is a retired postal worker and her mother a homemaker. McNellis's mental retardation became apparent early in her life. Although there was some social pressure to institutionalize her, her family was determined that she grow up at home. She attended day classes for mentally challenged children from ages four to six, but was removed when the repetitiveness of the classes eventually frustrated her. Her family decided that learning at home presented a wider range of opportunities, both social and artistic. From a time when she was very young it was evident to those around her that McNellis greatly enjoyed painting.

McNellis has been painting regularly, using tempera on blank newsprint as her medium, since childhood. For years her father brought home stacks of blank newsprint to keep up with the volume of her production. She still works only on this newsprint and has rejected any offers of canvas or better-quality paper.

Because she is nonliterate and her speech is understood only by family members, McNellis's paintings have become an extraordinary means of personal expression. Often a painting portrays an event from her day, and sometimes a series of works will develop from a particular event that has fascinated her. Her acute powers of observation enable her to depict eloquently the people, objects, and events she encounters every day. Her art makes it clear that McNellis sees a different, though in no way diminished, world.

McNellis has always painted late at night, frequently after everyone else in the house is asleep. She employs bold, rapid brushstrokes, and the wall near her desk is splattered with the by-products of this technique. She often draws the outline first with a colored felt marker or felt-tip pen, then fills in the works using inexpensive watercolor sets and tempera paint. She saves her empty paint containers and the shelves in her room are piled high with them.

When a painting is complete McNellis draws large letters across the bottom margin, sometimes cutting out the interiors of the O's. Cut out portions are occasionally part of the central picture. She generally trims each of the corners of a painting but is careful to preserve a fragment of the brightly rayed yellow sun that almost invariably appears in the upper right corner. Another recurring image in McNellis's work is the small fluffy clouds that line the top edge of each painting. When a piece is complete McNellis folds the piece into quarters and stores it. She is quick about this archiving, and has put many paintings away while they were still wet, leading to some sticking together. She appears to be less concerned about the fate of a finished picture than with the planning of her next.

UNTITLED (YELLOW DRESS), 1982
Tempera on paper sewing pattern
21″ × 27½″

UNTITLED (TRIANGLES), 1982
Tempera on paper
22″ × 28″

Laura Craig McNellis / 149

Anna Miller

(1906–)

Drawing mostly from memories of her past in rural Wisconsin, and occasionally from imagination and fantasy, Anna Miller has produced a body of strong and mysterious paintings. Her landscapes are charged with a brooding, animate drama.

Born Anna Louisa Flath in 1906 in Glenbeulah, Wisconsin, Miller began to paint in 1940 to pass the time while her husband, Lynn, worked as a night watchman in Milwaukee. She worked mostly in oil on canvas or masonite, creating large landscapes, portraits, and scenes from her everyday life.

After World War II, the Millers returned to her husband's birthplace of Augusta, Wisconsin, where Anna would spend the next three decades painting. After her husband's death in 1970, Miller virtually stopped painting and began having difficulty living alone on their isolated farm. Anxious about the fate of her paintings, worried that they might be "thrown out on a rubbish heap," in 1971 Miller donated over thirty pieces to the Art Department of Viterbo College in La Crosse, Wisconsin, where they are now on permanent display. Since 1976 Miller has lived in a nursing home in Eau Claire, Wisconsin.

OCTOBER STORM OF 1949, 1949
Oil on Masonite
24″ × 36″

Louis Monza

(1897–1984)

In 1938 Louis Monza was working as a housepainter in New York City when he fell from a scaffold and injured his back. A committed pacifist, he had also been watching the approach of war in Europe with trepidation, and during his convalescence, Monza began to express what he felt about these events in a symbolically rich and technically ambitious idiom. He came to regard himself as a professional, not a vocational, painter, and with the support of his wife, Heidi, whom he married in 1946, he was able to paint full time.

Monza responded strongly to historical events, from the horrors of World War II to the Three Mile Island disaster decades later. Yet his artistic sensibility, which is capable of blending the insights of Surrealism with the fractured perspectives of Cubism, is nourished by deeper sources.

Monza was born in the village of Turate, Italy, near Lake Como. At age seven he was apprenticed to the studio of a master furniture maker, where he learned to make pattern drawings as well as to carve wood. Monza approached his work with a draftsman's meticulousness. Village life seems to have instilled in Monza a "natural" Surrealism along with a strong anticlerical streak. He traveled to major European cities to work as a craftsman on a number of international expositions, an experience that seems to have sharpened his eye for detail and increased his compositional sophistication. In 1913 Monza came to the United States and found work as a railroad hand. In 1915 he made what would be the first of several trips to Mexico, where he encountered landscapes and artistic traditions that were both politically and formally inspiring. After Monza moved to California in 1946, the Mexican and Southwestern influences came to dominate his work.

Monza exhibited his paintings to favorable critical response at the Artists' Gallery in New York and other galleries in the 1940s and early 1950s, but he would wait almost thirty years for any wider recognition. In the meantime, living in Redondo Beach, California, he became a well-known figure in the flourishing South Bay artistic community, widely respected by more conventionally trained younger artists. In 1984 his work was included in a major show at the Long Beach Museum of Art.

UNTITLED, 1947
Oil on canvas
19½″ × 15½″

NAZI HOSPITAL, 1940
Oil on canvas
30" × 34"

Sister Gertrude Morgan

(1900–1980)

PRECIOUS LORD TAKE MY HAND
LEAD ME ON AND LET ME STAND,
1965–75
Tempera on board
14¾″ × 42″

"Satan is always just below your feet, looking for his chance, and you got to say, 'Get back! You low-down crawling devil . . .' "

Gertrude Morgan delivered that powerful message through hundreds of complex, biblically inspired paintings. She painted what could only be seen by the spirit—the saints' eternal home, the beast of Revelations, the New Jerusalem—with a conviction and detail that imply their unequivocal reality.

Gertrude Morgan's transformation into Sister Gertrude, bride of Christ and visionary communicator of gospel wisdom, began in Lafayette, Alabama, where she was raised as a Baptist. While in her thirties (she has given several dates for the experience), she was commanded by a voice to preach, and by 1939 she had come to New Orleans, where she would remain for the rest of her life. She preached on the city's streets for the next thirty years. She founded an orphanage and chapel, sang and played guitar, and, in 1956, began to paint. This expansion of her creativity was followed soon after by a vision that instructed Morgan to become a "bride of Christ." It was then that she forsook, in her gospel mission (including furniture and household objects) and in her dress, all colors but pure white. That whiteness became her trademark. At the same time, however, her painted world, comprising a spiritual autobiography of image and text, grew ever more vibrant and elaborate, with strong and symbolic color contrasts. Morgan used acrylics, inks, watercolors, pencils, and pastels to express both the joy of salvation and the perpetual struggle of human beings to triumph over Satan and his temptations.

NEW JERUSALEM, 24 ELDERS, 48 ANGELS, 1965–75
Gouache on cardboard
9″ × 9″

UNTITLED, 1965–75
Tempera on paper
11¼″ × 16¾″

Sister Gertrude Morgan / 157

UNTITLED, 1965–75
Tempera on paper board
17½″ × 12¾″

Edward ("Mr. Eddy") Mumma

(1908–1986)

In 1969 Ed Mumma, a truck farmer and junk dealer who had retired to Gaines-
ville, Florida, underwent an operation to remove his cataracts. As he was recovering, his daughter suggested he take an art course to occupy himself. At the
first class, the teacher criticized Mumma's work as sloppy. He never returned,
but set out painting on his own, eventually turning out nearly a thousand pictures. Before Mumma came to be known as Mr. Eddy—the nickname he gave
himself—he had tried several occupations. He was born in West Milton, Ohio,
near Cleveland, of Pennsylvania Dutch ancestry. He had little schooling and was
a hobo early in his life. Some years after he married, in 1937, he began to farm
corn, wheat, and soy beans, an occupation that lasted nearly a decade until he
began an antique and junk business. By the time he moved to Florida in 1966,
his wife had died, he no longer worked, and he drank heavily. After discovering
his vocation, Mumma painted steadily despite ill health—diabetes would eventually contribute to the loss of both his legs—but he rarely sold his work, and at his
death his small house was filled with nearly eight hundred paintings.

Mumma often took inspiration from images in a small collection of books
and magazines that he kept in his house (he painted his own version of the *Mona
Lisa* and a picture of van Gogh minus his ear); though capable of considerable
variety in his work, he concentrated on a single image. The vast majority of his
work consists of versions of a face and hands, rendered as an abstract set of
strong brushstrokes. Mumma ceaselessly varied the colors of this image, explor-
ing every conceivable combination. He painted with acrylics on a variety of
materials, from used canvases given him by art students at the nearby university
to wooden boards. Sometimes he painted on both sides of a work, and he produced at such a pace that the pictures often piled up before they had a chance to
dry. "I try to paint one a day," he used to remark.

UNTITLED, 1975–79
Oil on board
16″ × 12″

UNTITLED, 1970–80
Oil on canvas board
13½″ × 10⅝″

John ("J. B.") Murry

(1908–1988)

"When I started I prayed and prayed and the Lord sunk a vision from the sun. Everything I see is from the sun . . . I took the water and held it up to the sun and the sun came right to me . . ."

Such was one of the visions that came to J. B. Murry in the 1970s. He also reported seeing the reflection of an eagle flying across the sky in his doctor's eye, and he met a shadow version of his resurrected mother. His visions and other behavior raised questions about his sanity, and he was first jailed, then hospitalized for several weeks. After his release, he began to draw. The colorful and ghostly figurations of his work often include the other key feature of Murry's vision—spirit writing. The indecipherable script that sets up a strong rhythm in his work was dictated, according to Murry, directly by God. It could be read only by looking through a glass of the Lord's water, obtained from a well near his home in Glasoch County, Georgia, where Murry lived his entire life. He worked as a sharecropper and tenant farmer. He married in 1929 and left behind him at his death eleven children, sixteen grandchildren, thirteen great-grandchildren, and three great-great-grandchildren.

In addition to hundreds of drawings, with which he adorned his house, Murry produced pages of his spirit script and distributed them to members of his church congregation. Murry's ceremonial "readings" of his images often became powerful spiritual experiences. The drawings tantalize with a structure and a significance to which only Murry held the key.

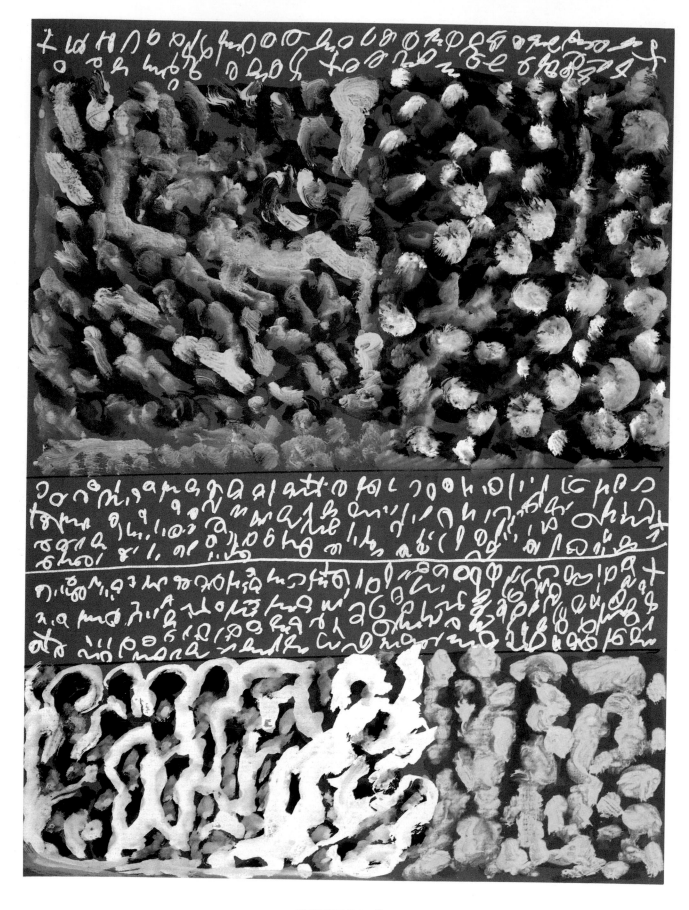

UNTITLED, 1987
Acrylic paintstick on paper
23″ × 18″

UNTITLED, 1986
Watercolor on paper
24″ × 18″

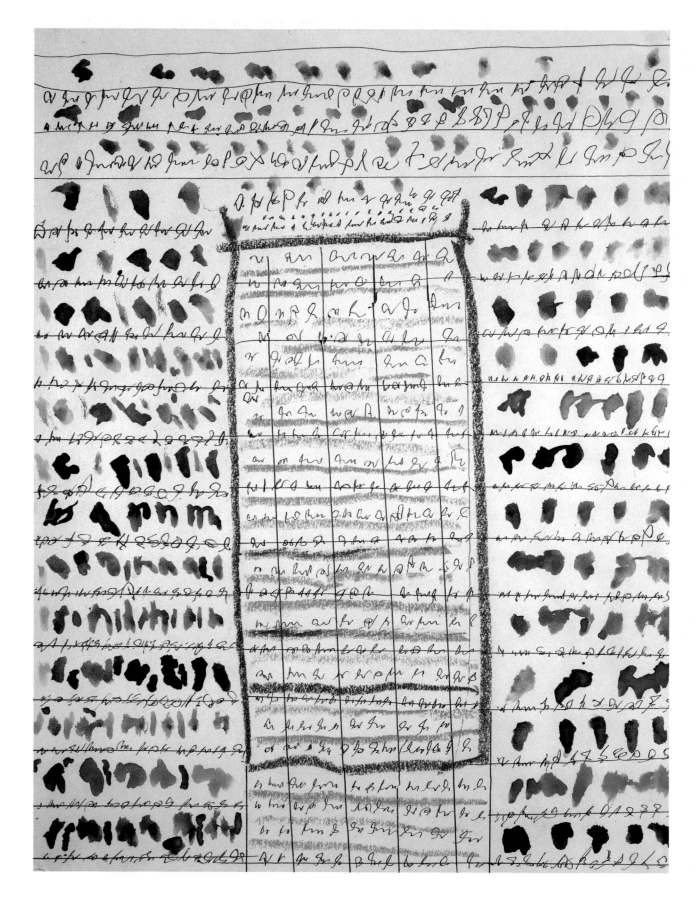

UNTITLED, 1984
Watercolor and wax crayon on paper
23½″ × 18″

UNTITLED, 1985–86
Tempera on paper
28″ × 22″

John Murry / 165

William Oleksa

(1956–)

Bill Oleksa began to draw and paint only relatively recently. Born into a Polish-American family on Long Island, Oleksa attended college but had no formal training in or contact with art—and no apparent interest in it—until he participated briefly in a hospital art class in the mid-1980s. In 1987 he began to create his large, cartoonlike paintings, with their simple single images composed of zones of pure primary colors. (Oleksa has a deep aversion to mixing his colors.) Yet he drew his inspiration not from comic books or cartoons but from the people and objects in the world around him. Each of his paintings he planned carefully and executed by following drawings he had done beforehand. After two and a half years, however, as suddenly as the impulse to paint had arisen, it ceased, and Oleksa stopped painting. He has recently resumed in a very different vein, fashioning constructions from pieces of foam core, which he cuts and glues together according to his unique geometric sense, and then paints.

UNTITLED, 1988
Acrylic on paper
22¼″ × 30″

UNTITLED, 1988
Acrylic on paper
22¼″ × 30″

UNTITLED, 1988
Acrylic on paper
22¼" × 30"

UNTITLED, 1988
Acrylic on paper
22¼″ × 30″

John W. Perates

(1895–1970)

As a boy in Amphikleia in the Greek islands, John Perates became familiar with the Byzantine-influenced art of religious icons. Their stylized and rigid figural treatment would serve as the primary model for his own work, whose forms Perates combined with others in which he perceived deep affinities, especially styles of New England funerary representation.

In Greece, Perates had been trained in wood carving by his grandfather, and after emigrating to Portland, Maine, in 1912, he went to work as a cabinet-maker and developed his skills working with such hardwoods as maple, oak, and walnut. By 1930 Perates was able to establish his own cabinetry shop. When business was slow, he built furniture for the local Greek Orthodox church. Through this connection, he soon began work on a massive project that would occupy the next forty years of his life—a series of painted relief carvings depicting aspects of Christ's life, his disciples, and the Holy Family. The work included panels as well as a pulpit, a sixteen-foot altar, and a bishop's throne. Perates devoted as much attention to coloring the panels with his own unusual palette of rich but subdued tones, as to carving them, and he varnished each panel to preserve its surface and color. Up to half a foot thick and in several cases more than six feet tall, the panels were so monumental that most of them were never used in the church, and after Perates's death they were discovered in the church's basement.

ST. ANDREW, 1940
Enamel on wood relief carving
49½″ × 28″

ST. PETER AND PAUL, 1940
Painted wood relief
74″ × 38½″

Benjamin ("B. F.") Perkins

(1904–1993)

The paintings and painted gourds that crowd the second floor of the Reverend B. F. Perkins's house in western Alabama are part of an environment that includes the Hartline Assembly Church of God, where Perkins preaches, the Hartline education building, and a replica of the tomb of Christ. All this and his painting, too, Perkins began after the age of sixty-two.

Perkins grew up in rural Alabama and, he says, at seventeen joined the Marine Corps for which he was sent on "secret missions." He later attended the University of Virginia, where he reports that he majored in "Hebrew history" but also studied preaching and engineering. In 1929 he was ordained a minister in the Assembly of God and in 1940 joined the Church of God, in which he became a bishop. Perkins married, fathered two daughters, and worked as a safety engineer at National Airport in Washington, D.C. After he and his wife were divorced, he moved back to Alabama and started his church. When it burned down, he built another. And when the Church of God tried to transfer him to Arkansas, he fought a seven-year battle with the national church organization. He was finally forced to rename the church, which today has about twenty parishioners.

In 1979 Perkins began contemplating retirement and began painting, he says, "to keep from sitting down and doing nothing." He was inspired to paint on gourds that he saw being sold along the roadside and took occasional art classes at Albert Brewer Junior College in Fayette. Perkins has all but retired from preaching, which has allowed him to concentrate on his painting. His themes are American history and patriotic imagery, biblical stories, and heavily patterned interpretations of objects "from the tomb of King Tut." A stone he once carved during his battle with the Church of God expresses his personal credo: "I have only two hands and one life. I cannot give more and will not give less. Benjamin F. Perkins."

USA—HOME OF THE BRAVE,
LAND OF THE FREE, 1987
Acrylic on metal
29" × 56"

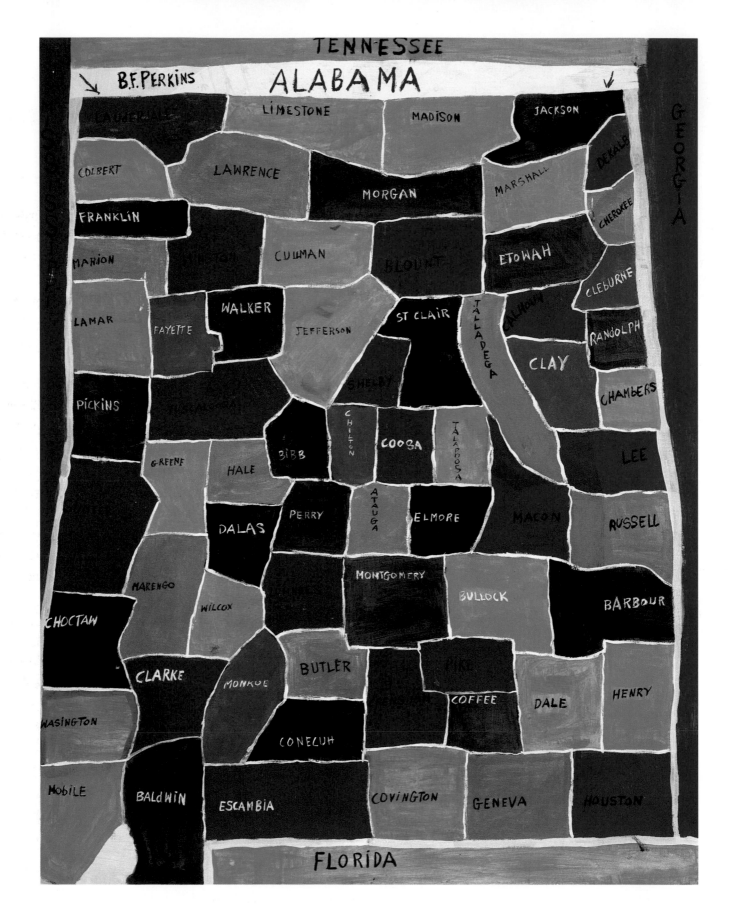

ALABAMA, 1989
Oil on canvas
60" × 48"

Elijah Pierce

(1892–1984)

Central and southern Ohio have proved to be fertile ground for self-taught artists, including the late William Hawkins and the sculptor Popeye Reed. One of the most important was Elijah Pierce—preacher, barber, and creator of painted reliefs in wood.

Pierce was born near Baldwyn, Mississippi. His father was an ex-slave and a church deacon. Early on Pierce developed a distaste for the hard labor of farming. He learned to barber at sixteen and soon opened his own shop. He would practice the trade off and on all his life. For a half dozen years after his first wife died, in 1917, Pierce worked on bridge gangs and rode the rails, carving wood with a pocket knife in his spare time. Once run out of town by a lynch mob, he moved north in the early 1920s, first to Illinois, then to Columbus, Ohio, where he settled. After he received a religious calling and was ordained a preacher, he turned his talents to creating multipaneled painted carvings, such as a monumental crucifixion, to illustrate his sermons. "Every piece of wood I carve is a message, a sermon," he once remarked.

But religious subjects formed only part of his work. Making his own rough frames and using enamel paints, Pierce also painted scenes from his own life, fables, historical incidents, animals, and portraits of such contemporary figures as boxer Joe Louis.

In 1954 Pierce built his own barbershop on Long Street in Columbus and began to hang his work there. He gradually became better known as an artist than a barber, and renamed the shop the Elijah Pierce Art Gallery. After his death the shop was sold and the building torn down, but the Columbus Museum of Art acquired a substantial collection of the reliefs.

HORSE RACING, 1928
Polychromed wood
24" × 8¾"

GOD'S PLENTY, 1973
Polychromed wood
23″ × 14¾″

UNTITLED, 1970—72
Carved, polychromed wood with glitter
16″ × 17¾″

Horace Pippin

(1888–1946)

My opinion of art is that a man should have love for it, because my idea is that he paints from his heart and mind. To me it seems impossible for another to teach one of Art

—Horace Pippin

One of the major figures of self-taught painting in this century, Horace Pippin was born in West Chester, Pennsylvania, and began to draw in early childhood. While still attending school he entered a correspondence art contest and, much to his delight, won a set of colored crayons and a box of dry watercolors and brushes. He worked on a farm from the age of fourteen, loaded coal and worked other odd jobs until joining the army in 1917—perhaps the pivotal event of his life. Throughout this time Pippin continued to draw and keep sketchbooks. During World War I, while serving in France, he was wounded in battle and lost much of the use of his right arm. There, he won the Croix de Guerre, France's highest award for bravery.

Upon returning to the United States Pippin was spurred by the impact of what he had seen and felt during the war to paint his first significant picture. Gradually regaining the use of his injured arm, he worked long days and was supported by his wife, who took in laundry, while Pippin helped with the deliveries.

He was discovered by Dr. Christian Brinton, who arranged for his first show in West Chester in 1937. Later, he came to the attention of collector Dr. Albert Barnes and gained increasing fame from the inclusion of his pictures in the 1938 landmark exhibition "Masters of Popular Painting" at the Museum of Modern Art. He studied briefly at the Barnes Foundation in Philadelphia and was exposed to the painterly values of the Impressionist paintings in its collection, but he preferred to work on his own rather than study in a traditional fashion. By 1939 he was represented by the Robert Carlen Gallery in Philadelphia and was well known to collectors and the public.

Much of Pippin's work embodies a deep appreciation of both the ordinary and the heroic in American history and daily life. There is a quiet strength to Pippin's simple and personal style of painting. He used a simple palette of colors and took extreme care in composition. He was at work on an ambitious cycle of religious paintings at the time of his death.

THE GETAWAY, 1939
Oil on canvas
24″ × 35½″

John Podhorsky

(ACTIVE CA. 1950S)

John Podhorsky's drawings present a dense and intricate psychological self-portrait. Architectural, mechanical, animal, and human images, rendered in a spidery hand, are crowded and sometimes overlaid with text that labels and often elaborately describes them. Podhorsky's drawings are not discrete productions but, like walls covered with graffiti, complex records of different experiences, preoccupations, recollections, and plans. In Podhorsky's world, it is not enough simply to see things. Each subject, whether it is a goose being shot, a diagram of a water propeller, or a bridge, must be labeled, explained, and organized in order to confirm its reality.

Nonetheless, as close as these drawings bring us to the inner workings of an imagination, the man who created them remains almost a complete mystery. Podhorsky's work came to public view, as did Martin Ramírez's (page 185) and P. M. Wentworth's (page 261), through the northern California psychologist, artist, and art historian, Dr. Tarmo Pasto. It is likely that Pasto met Podhorsky at one of the psychiatric institutions where the former worked, probably De Witt State Hospital, where Martin Ramírez was also confined. Podhorsky's wife was also institutionalized and she too made art, partially in response to the interest shown in her husband's work. Podhorsky was actively employed in California during the 1950s as a carpenter and woodworker.

From the compulsively detailed and linear drawings Podhorsky produced, one can speculate that he may have worked for a company supplying architectural elements by mail order to builders. Indeed, from Podhorsky's eccentric descriptions of his houses, bridges, and machines, it often seems as if he had actually planned to build the structures in his drawings.

HOUSE ELEVATION, 1960
Colored pencil on paper
18″ × 24″

UNTITLED, 1960
Pencil and crayon on paper
18⅜″ × 24″

Lamont Alfred ("Old Ironsides") Pry

(1921–1987)

SELF PORTRAIT, LAST ROUNDUP,
1960
Enamel on wood
12″ × 17½″

For much of his life, Lamont Pry was fascinated by circuses and especially by acts featuring the most death-defying feats. Although he painted a variety of subjects, including many pictures of World War I aircraft, his most ambitious and distinctive works record the manifold and spectacular acts of the circuses he knew. In these pictures, organized much like advertising posters, Pry's own name figures prominently.

Pry was born in Mauch Chunk, Pennsylvania, near Allentown, and left home in his late teens with the intention of joining a circus, as his father had. In his paintings Pry imagines himself performing all manner of dangerous aerial acrobatic acts, but it appears he never achieved the success in the circus he shows on canvas, and may not even have joined one. His sobriquet came not from a circus feat but a real-life one: during World War II Pry miraculously survived the crash of his B-25 bomber, which gained him the nickname Old Ironsides.

Immediately after the war Pry joined the civil service and was employed as a hospital orderly until a heart condition forced him into retirement and into a nursing home in 1968. He began to paint soon afterward, using cardboard, poster paint, house paint, enamel, metallic paint, and ink. His circus pictures depict and explain with text many of the acts Pry had seen or participated in. Pry also used the paintings to address the audience with ideas and exhortations. The lively activity of these paintings illustrates the truth of the statement he was fond of visually quoting: "There's no business like show business."

THE GREAT HOXIE BROTHERS CIRCUS, 1960–62
Enamel on paper
20⅞″ × 27⅞″

Martin Ramírez

(1885–1963)

The Mexican poet and philosopher Octavio Paz has said of Martin Ramírez, "He is neither a precursor nor a predecessor: he is a symbol." Ramírez's life offers an emblematic image of the artist's will to communicate at all costs, against the most difficult obstacles. Most of what is known about his life comes from a psychologist, Dr. Tarmo Pasto, and not from the artist's own lips. For sometime around 1915, according to Pasto, Ramírez ceased to speak at all.

The exact location of Ramírez's birthplace in the state of Jalisco in west central Mexico is unknown, but his drawings contain many clues, including details of landscape and images of local saints who were worshipped. Likewise, little is known about his family, which he left early in the century when he went north to California in search of work. He found it probably as a railroad section hand, and trains became a central symbol in his drawings. The difficult conditions of his life and something like cultural shock seem to have sent him into a long fall. In 1930 he was picked up as a derelict in a Los Angeles park, diagnosed as schizophrenic, and institutionalized. He would spend the rest of his life at De Witt State Hospital, where he died in 1963.

According to Dr. Pasto, who exhibited Ramírez's work to art students in classes he taught at Sacramento State University, Ramírez began drawing around 1940, but the attendants destroyed his work. Around 1948 Ramírez managed to pass some three hundred drawings to Dr. Pasto and passed others to fellow inmates at the institution. Most were made on paper bags or scraps of paper glued together with a paste made of potatoes and bread and his own saliva. Later Dr. Pasto provided high-quality materials.

Ramírez's images enforce a relentless framing order in the strong parallel lines of enclosing hills, doorways, and tunnels. Yet at the heart of each enclosure lies an image—a saint, a deer, a cross—that has been transformed into a mythic sign of purity, power, or separation. In 1989 an exhibition in Mexico City acknowledged Ramírez as a major twentieth-century Latin American artist.

UNTITLED, 1954
Pencil, tempera, crayon, and collage on
paper
36″ × 90¼″

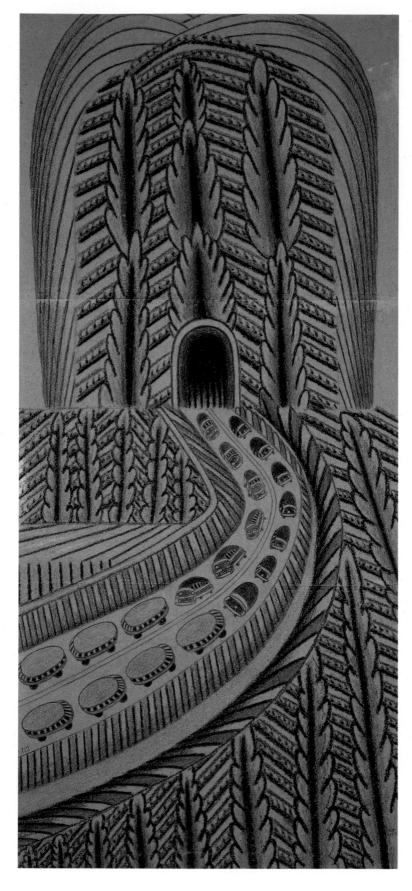

UNTITLED, 1954
Colored pencil on paper
53½″ × 24″

UNTITLED, 1950
Mixed media on paper
32″ × 19¼″

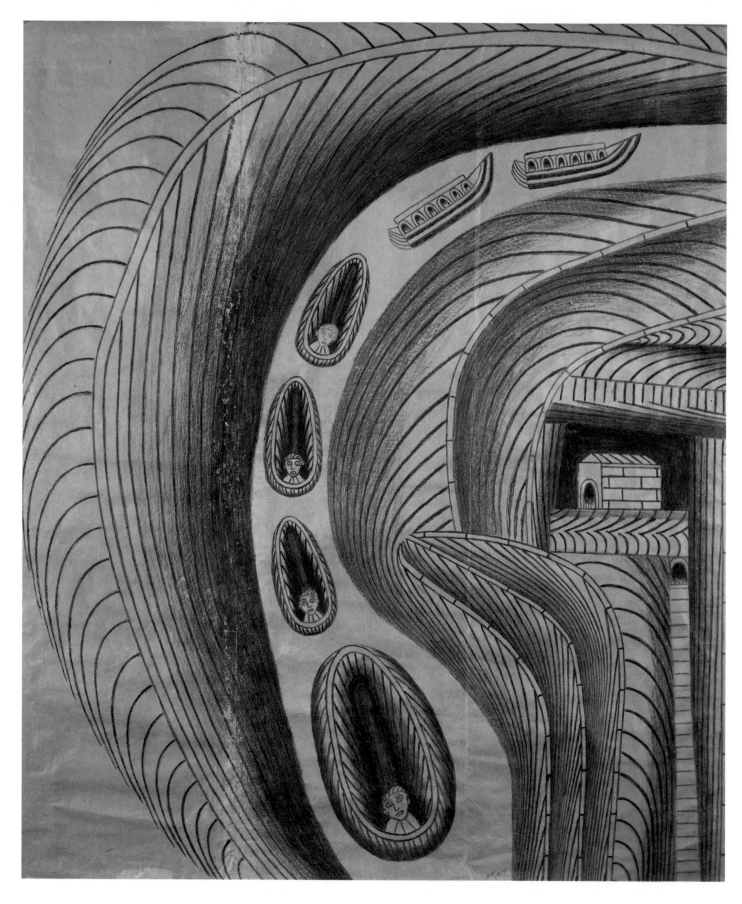

UNTITLED, 1954
Pencil, tempera, and crayon on paper
53″ × 43¼″

UNTITLED, 1950
Mixed media on paper
35″ × 24″

UNTITLED, 1955
Crayon on paper
44½″ × 32¼″

J. Richardson

(ACTIVE CA. 1917–1922)

Eighty-five drawings, sealed with evident attention in a crafted black poplar box that first appeared at a country auction, represent almost all that is known of the J. Richardson who created and signed them. Lettering on some of the paintings also indicates that Richardson worked in the Massachusetts seacoast town of New Bedford, and his careful dating of the work makes it fairly certain that he did the majority of the drawings between 1917 and 1922. Experts who have examined the drawings have speculated that they may have been done as part of a program of art therapy, which first began to gain acceptance around the time of World War I. Many of the drawings represent nautical scenes and specific ships that Richardson might well have seen in New Bedford harbor. Others depict Boston scenes, episodes from the Civil War, personages from the early history of the United States, and contemporary views including dirigibles and airplanes.

HULL, England. August 24, Sept. 1921
Graphite and colored pencil on paper
30" × 22"

TENNESSEE CONFEDERATES, Dec. 1920
Graphite and colored pencil on paper
30″ × 22″

Achilles G. Rizzoli

(1896–1981)

In the San Francisco architecture firm where A. G. Rizzoli worked for many years, he was regarded as a competent draftsman. It is doubtful that any of his colleagues in the firm had any notion of the other side of Achilles Rizzoli.

From the mid-1930s to the mid-1940s, Rizzoli produced thirty-five pen and ink drawings, including portraits, mostly of his mother, modeled on examples in a "Learn to Draw" book. Another set of images from this time, spectacular Art Deco architectural renderings, herald the work that would occupy him for the rest of his life: thousands of drawings of monumental buildings, part of a plan for a community mysteriously designated only as "Y.T.T.E."

These pencil drawings were made on large sheets of architectural tracing paper divided into eight sections, each containing a drawing, poem, prose quotation, commemoration of an event—the burning of a church, for instance—tribute to a person, or some combination of these. Rizzoli was fascinated with the idea of euthanasia, and many of his structures appear to be gigantic death chambers. He made up his own language, replete with many symbolically loaded solecisms ("carchitecturally," for example). The drawings and writings document a life lived, in Rizzoli's words, "in an unbelievably hermetically sealed spherical inalienable maze of light and sound seeing imagery expand in every direction."

Rizzoli was born in northern California and lived most of his life in San Francisco. His father committed suicide in Italy in 1915 and Rizzoli shared a home with his mother, to whom he was devoted, until her death in 1937. Rizzoli was obsessed with his mother; after her death he maintained her room exactly as she left it. He never married. Rizzoli had little formal education, but at the age of seventeen or eighteen he trained for two years as a draftsman at a technical school in the Bay area. In the 1920s and 1930s he wrote half a dozen nearly incoherent novels and short stories. Unable to find publishers for any of them, he carefully saved all his rejection notices.

Rizzoli sometimes held open houses to present his artwork and poems "to the public." The few people who attended were sometimes honored for their patronage by being given large works in color. In 1976 Rizzoli suffered a debilitating stroke and was forced to move from his home. He died five years later.

MOTHER SYMBOLICALLY RECAPTURED, 1937
Colored ink on paper
30″ × 50″

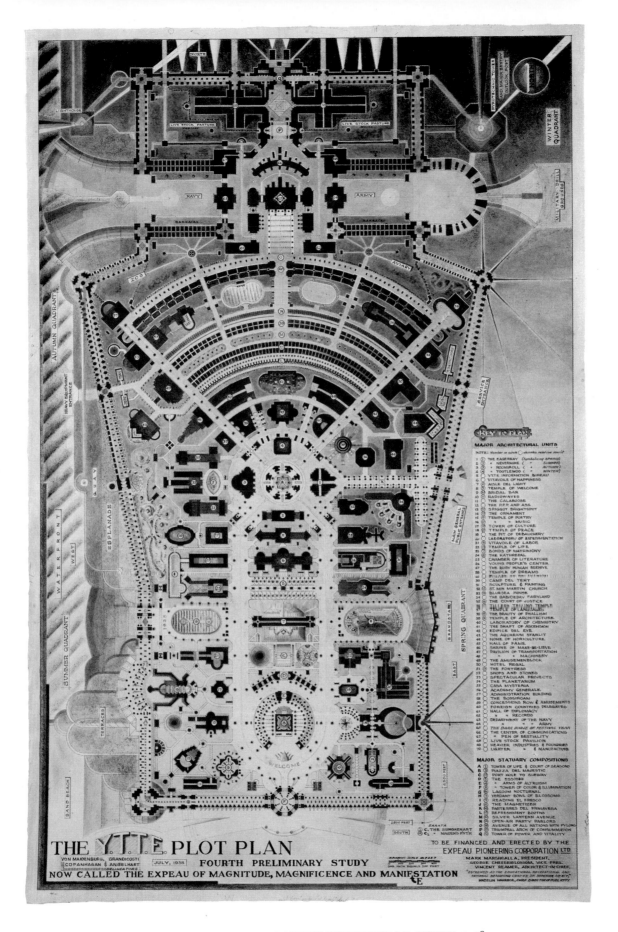

Y.T.T.E. PLOT PLAN—FOURTH PRELIMINARY STUDY, 1938
Colored ink on paper
24″ × 13″

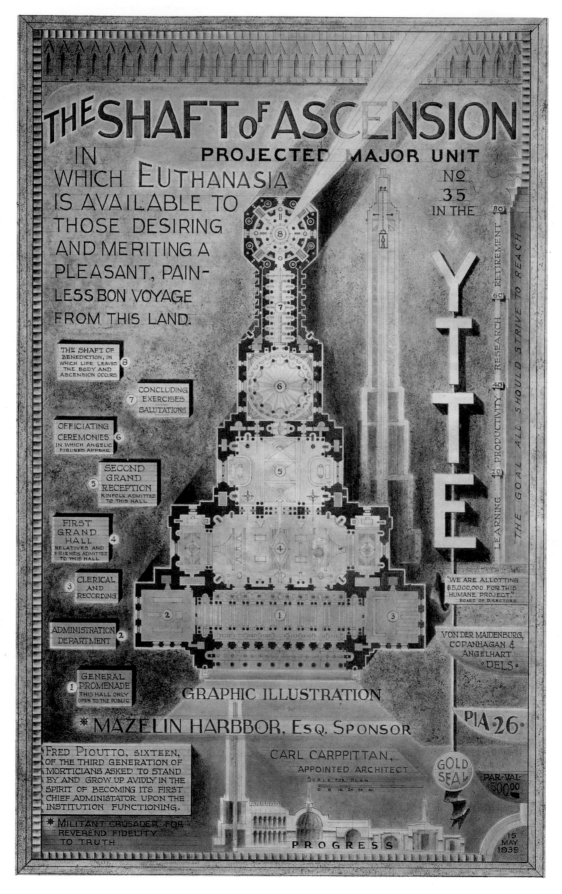

SHAFT OF ASCENSION, May 15, 1939
Colored ink on paper
21" × 13"

Royal Robertson

(1936–)

ARTIST-LIBRA-PROPHET, ARTISTICO, and PATRIARCHAL ROYAL proclaim a few of the signs that adorn the house of Royal Robertson in southern Louisiana. The signs also warn away prostitutes, pushers, and other evildoers and, perhaps most vehemently, fulminate against the woman who Robertson believes betrayed him—his wife of some twenty years, Adell. Her departure in the mid-1970s provoked an outpouring of signs and drawings that transformed Robertson's house into an environment and signaled the beginning of his estrangement from the surrounding community. Robertson claims that he started drawing when the Lord commanded him to denounce the evil ways of women. Robertson remains tormented by this event and by an accompanying fear of forces as diverse as the Mafia and beings from outer space.

Robertson was born in St. Mary Parish, Louisiana, and left high school to work first as a field hand and later as apprentice to a sign painter, where he most certainly learned some of his technique. He claims to have traveled while in his twenties to North Dakota and California and to have worked for Martin Luther King, Jr. In 1978, after his wife left him, he enrolled briefly in a correspondence art course.

Robertson's drawings are at once angry and as precise as a cartoon. Some of them take sexual horror as their theme. All of them are informed by an architectural sense of draftsmanship, especially those that depict futuristic buildings. Robertson works in pen, crayon, enamels, and felt marker on poster board, and all his images are accompanied by references to biblical texts.

THE GIANT HAS RISEN, 1978–80
Tempera and pencil on paper
19″ × 26″

Nellie Mae Rowe

(1900—1982)

SHOPPING IN VINNING,
1981
Mixed media on paper
17⅞″ × 23⅝″

Nellie Mae Rowe's greatest gift was her instinctive understanding of the relation between color and form. She used crayons and acrylics to create boldly chromatic backgrounds for images of animals and country scenes. All the elements of her paintings find their space in the same plane, and on that plane it is color that provides rhythm and depth.

Rowe began drawing at an early age. She learned to make voodoolike dolls and sculpted and painted heads, as well as quilts, wood sculptures, and other decorative objects, from her mother, the wife of a farmer and blacksmith in rural Fayette County, Georgia. Here Rowe grew up with nine siblings. By the time she reached 16, however, the rigors of farm life had become intolerable, and she ran away to marry her first husband. In 1930 she moved to Vinings, near Atlanta, where she worked as a domestic. In 1939 she and her second husband built a one-story cottage in Vinings where Rowe lived until her death. She called the home her playhouse, and in 1948 she began to festoon it and its small lot with dolls, sculptures, and found objects, a practice that for years brought her into conflict with some members of the community. In her early sixties Rowe began a creative outpouring of dolls, drawings, sculptures, and paintings. As she once remarked, "Drawing is the only thing I think is good for the Lord. When I wake up in glory, I want to hear, 'Well done, Nellie, well done.' "

REAL GIRL, 1980
Crayon and pencil on paper with photo collage
13½″ × 11″

GREEN HORSE, 1980
Wax crayon and pencil on paper
16″ × 20″

UNTITLED, 1981
Wax crayon and pencil on paper
18″ × 24″

UNTITLED, 1981
Wax crayon and pencil on paper
37″ × 36″

Ellis W. Ruley

(1882–1959)

When Ellis Ruley, who was black, was found dead on a road near his home in Norwich, Connecticut, the death was ruled accidental, from a fall and subsequent exposure. But many in the area suspected foul play, with racial motives, because Ruley's art showed whites and blacks, men and women, dancing and performing together in a provocative and mysterious Garden of Eden.

Ruley was born and lived his entire life in Norwich. He and his wife, who was white, were married in 1924 and had one child. Ruley most likely began to paint after his retirement from his job driving a concrete truck, about ten years before his death. Comparatively few of his paintings have come into circulation, yet they had earned Ruley something of a local reputation and a place in the Norwich Museum well before his death.

This may be due at least as much to their themes as to Ruley's technical competence: he explored conjunctions of race and sexuality at a time when almost no visual artists in America even acknowledged such themes. Ruley's Garden of Eden is a languorous yet ominous place, where seminude women and men, white and black, display and disport themselves. In all of these works viewers themselves are implicated as voyeurs.

UNTITLED, 1940–50
Oil on paper
21¼″ × 27¾″

THE CIRCUS ACT, 1940–50
Oil on cardboard
27" × 21"

UNTITLED, 1940—50
Enamel on Masonite
22½″ × 24¼″

Anthony Joseph Salvatore
(1938–)

Many self-taught artists have been "called" to testify in the Christian faith, but few have yoked their talent so rigorously to the scriptures as Joseph Salvatore, who was directed by the Lord to illustrate all sixty-six books of the Bible. Yet what emerges from his paintings, each of which is marked on the back with the verse numbers it illustrates, is neither sermon nor instruction but the spiritual reinterpretation of the Bible by a creative intelligence.

Joseph Salvatore was born in Youngstown, Ohio, to an immigrant cement worker with a talent for sidewalk drawing. The father encouraged the son, who as a child took Saturday art classes and in 1978 took courses as a sometime art student at Youngstown State. He also studied the Bible through correspondence courses. In the interim, pivotal events occurred. The first was Salvatore's conversion at age twenty to the Pentecostal faith; he eventually became an ordained Pentecostal minister. The other was the deterioration of his physical health. At sixteen he was removed from school for fainting spells and at thirty-five was involved in a serious auto accident. Injuries from the accident and other illnesses eventually sent him to a nursing home in 1973, where he began to paint in earnest and his work was first exhibited.

According to Salvatore's teachers, his style was formed before he arrived at the university. In the visions that come to him in prayer, Salvatore receives not only the knowledge of which verses to illustrate but also the full-color articulation of the scenes themselves. He has developed a fluid, organic, and color-dense style, using pencil, acrylic, and rubbed crayon. Sometimes the paint is built up to fifteen layers, with wax encaustic added as he paints, and the final product is covered with hair spray. The paintings support a complex symbolic vocabulary that enables him to conflate several verses into one "story," which he also supplements by his own reading of history and biblical commentary. Like all great Christian artists, Salvatore works on three planes at once: personal vision, historical reality, and sacred text.

UNTITLED, 1983
Oil pastel, acrylic, and mixed media on paper
24″ × 18″

UNTITLED, 1983
Oil, pastel, acrylic, and mixed media on paper
18″ × 24″

John ("Jack") Savitsky

Coal mining, so much a part of this nation's mythology, has often been dealt with in folk song but rarely in the visual arts. Perhaps the most notable example is the work of Jack Savitsky, known as Coal Miner Jack. Savitsky was born in the coal town of Silver Creek, Pennsylvania, and has lived all his life in coal-mining country. He went to work at fifteen and entered the mines at eighteen. He first began to draw with chalk on the sides of the mine tunnels. Although he sometimes painted signs and murals for local barrooms in return for gasoline and cigarettes, this avocation did not develop into anything more substantial until black lung, the endemic disease of coal miners, forced him to stop work in 1959. At this time the mines in Lansford, Pennsylvania, where Savitsky was living, closed. He could see them from the small second-floor room of his house as he painted, and painting for him became a form of recollection as well as recreation.

Almost all of Savitsky's paintings, done with oil and acrylic on a variety of surfaces, including canvas board and Masonite, and on paper with watercolors, colored pencils, crayon, and pen, deal with the lives of coal miners. He often borders a central image with a series of vignettes that amplify the picture's subject. The picture of the life that emerges from Savitsky's very simple and bright images is at once unvarnished and dignified. The stooped postures and often sad or blank expressions of his people are balanced by a stolid strength. Savitsky painted for eleven years, selling his work locally at flea markets with the help of his wife, before he gained wider recognition.

MADONNA AND CHILD, 1964
Pencil and crayon on paper
9″ × 12″

Jon Serl

(1894–)

Outspoken and intensely individualistic, Jon Serl has embraced many careers in his lifetime. Serl's paintings, with their hollow-eyed men and women, evoke a powerful sense of the ceremonial and dramatic; this may spring in part from Serl's early career as a vaudeville actor and female impersonator. Serl was born Joseph Searles at Olean, on an Indian reservation in upstate New York, into a vaudeville family of thirteen. His parents put him on stage when he was ten.

His career as a performer came to a halt when his father fell ill, and the family moved west in 1915, but by the early 1930s, Serl had found work in Hollywood as an actor, dancer, and scriptwriter. When he saw a horse killed in an accident on a film set, he has said, he decided to leave Hollywood for good. He moved to San Juan Capistrano, where many friends from the film community, such as Hedda Hopper, came to visit.

Serl has offered a number of accounts of his beginnings as an artist. One version has it that he began just after World War II, when he needed a picture to decorate a room of his house. He painted portraits on his window shades and hasn't stopped since. As he says, "I paint all day every day." In 1971 he moved abruptly to Lake Elsinore, a small town north of San Diego, and, on the edge of poverty, constructed the twenty-five room "house" that contains his books, his dogs, and a large number of the more than 1,400 paintings he has done. Though Serl's output has been prodigious, his emotional investment in the work has been equally great. As he says, "The most difficult part is when you have to sign a painting and admit that it's yours. Then you have to rake up everything in you and ask, Is this what I wanted?"

UNTITLED, 1978–82
Oil on board
35⅜″ × 23¼″

UNTITLED, 1974–78
Oil on board
48″ × 60″

UNTITLED, 1972–75
Oil on board
34″ × 21¼″

Drossos P. Skyllas

(1912–1973)

In the work of Drossos Skyllas, classical principles are wedded to a highly idiosyncratic vision. Skyllas, who was born on the Greek island of Kalymnos, was exposed to classical and orthodox iconic influences as he grew up. In his paintings, Skyllas strove to reproduce only what he saw. The result was carefully structured, stereotypically imagined compositions. Yet the painter's style transcends his formulas. Everything is captured in a timeless present, seen face on, with equal—and portentous—clarity. Like the photo-realists of a later time, Skyllas also sought to hide every trace of a painted surface. He often made his own brushes because he couldn't buy brushes fine enough to create the smooth surfaces he sought.

Skyllas did little painting in Greece, working instead in the tobacco business owned by his father, who opposed Skyllas's artistic inclinations. He came to Chicago with his wife after World War II and began his career as an artist. Supported by his wife, who believed in his talent, Skyllas haunted the Chicago Art Institute, advertised himself as a portrait painter, and even had his work exhibited in Chicago. But Skyllas saw the prices paid for works by Frank Stella, who in Skyllas's opinion painted "only lines." Skyllas thought his own work deserved as much and set prices so high that no customers responded. Skyllas worked slowly and painstakingly and produced only thirty-five paintings in his lifetime, including portraits, nudes, still lifes, and landscapes—all, as he said, "only pure, realistic paintings, one hundred percent like photographs."

SUNRISE (DIANNA) REFLECTION,
1950–53
Oil on canvas
42″ × 50″

THREE SISTERS, 1950–53
Oil on canvas
58″ × 39″

MADONNA, 1960–65
Oil on canvas
66″ × 47¾″

GIRL WITH CAT, 1960
Oil on canvas
26″ × 20″

WISCONSIN CAVE, 1950
Oil on canvas
24″ × 30″

Mary Tillman Smith

(1904–)

Around 1978 Mary T. Smith began to transform the one-acre yard surrounding her home in the town of Hazelhurst, Mississippi, into a highly public form of spiritual autobiography. Here she has catalogued the revelations and figures of her inner life. She created her outdoor portrait gallery on pieces of plywood and corrugated tin, using only one or two colors for each picture. Some of the pictures represent farm animals, but most contain images of local people, sometimes allegorized, such as "Mr. Beg" (Big), and other human figures rendered in an elemental style that recalls West African ceremonial masks. These powerful presences are interspersed with designs, signs, and slogans that proclaim Mary T. Smith's relation to God and the world. THE LORD MY HART, says one. HERE I AM, reads another, and DON'T YOU SEE ME.

Before the world began to "see" her through her art, Smith worked as a tenant farmer, gardener, and household domestic. She married twice. She began artistic work in earnest—to "tidy up her yard" as she says—after she retired in the mid-1970s. Since then, Smith has been indefatigable in creating, maintaining, and encouraging others to visit the site, though recently many of her paintings have been sold or removed from the yard. In 1985 Smith suffered a stroke; her speech and writing were impaired, but this only temporarily interfered with her artistic output of up to two pictures a day.

UNTITLED, 1986
Enamel on tin
30″ × 30″

Mary Tillman Smith / 221

UNTITLED, 1986—88
Enamel on wood panel
33″ × 24″

UNTITLED, 1988
Enamel on tin
65½″ × 27″

UNTITLED, 1987—88
Enamel on wood
25″ × 23½″

UNTITLED, 1987
Enamel on wood panel
28" × 60"

Matthew Ivan Smith

(1938–)

In Matthew I. Smith's precise interrogations of reality, the natural world he confronts is only a starting point. With an almost mathematical rigor, Smith will often "analyze" the same scene—whether a tree or an audience ring at the Metropolitan Opera—from slightly different distances and perspectives, as if each change forced him to reconfirm the reality of the subject.

Smith was born in New York City into an unusually talented family. His grandfather was the composer Ernest Bloch; his mother was a student of Nadia Boulanger and a pioneer of old music; and his father a distinguished topological mathematician. Smith's drawings show evidence of all these talents. Even before the age of eight, when Smith first began to fill small notebooks with precisely remembered images, his parents recognized that he was artistically and musically gifted—but learning-impaired. For the next two decades, Smith, who lives with his family, endured the sometimes contradictory diagnoses and recommendations of various specialists, all the while producing hundreds of precise crayon (and later acrylic) renderings of his world. Smith has always focused on the visual patterns of his subjects, patterns of both form and color. Around 1975, however, his vision began to mature and gain both expressive range and flexibility. It was then that he, in his words, "joined reality," and his experience of the world became more intimate. Though Smith has created disconcerting portraits, he rarely paints faces. He seems to prefer, instead, the formal symmetries and conundrums of perspective presented by nature—whether present or recollected. Years after the event, for example, he returned to memories of a family trip, to fashion precise images of the American West.

UNTITLED, 1974
Crayon on paper
17¾" × 23¾"

Simon Sparrow

(1925–)

"There is no present that you can see in my work," says Simon Sparrow. "The glitter? I see the same thing back in the A.D." By A.D., however, Sparrow means B.C., and his work seeks a timelessness that transcends the ages. Simon Sparrow is, in fact, a practitioner of the ancient art of mosaic. He also draws, but it is his glass assemblages that have earned him recognition as an artist. The resurrection of this art, carrying associations with the decorative splendor of the past—associations of which Sparrow is very much aware—gives his images their power.

Sparrow's "palette" consists of almost anything small that is capable of reflecting light: beads, shells, costume jewelery, china, shards of glass, even broken watches. In a process of spiritual synthesis, these bits and pieces are glued on panels to form iconic wholes.

Sparrow lives and works in Madison, Wisconsin, on whose streets he has often exhibited his work and preached his own version of the Pentecostal faith, which he terms "holy" as opposed to merely "religious." As a child of seven, Sparrow recalls, he began drawing in the dirt with a stick and preaching to animals in the woods around his home in rural North Carolina, where he moved at age two from West Africa. His father was African, he says, his mother Cherokee, and he sees himself as a link between African and Native American cultures. When he was twelve, Sparrow left home for Philadelphia, where he was raised by a Jewish family. He worked as a dishwasher before enlisting in the army, where he boxed. Twice married and the father of eight, he moved to Madison in the late 1960s. There he still works in a small room of his house, crowded with drawings and materials. Sparrow regards himself as a conduit for the holy spirit, which speaks through his art. "When I'm doing a picture," he says, "I feel like I'm in another time, another world, all at once, just like that."

UNTITLED, 1983
Mixed media
30″ × 60″

WOMAN WITH BLUE BREASTS, 1987
Mixed media
44½″ × 32″ × 3″

Henry Speller

(1900–)

The world of Henry Speller's drawings is one of bright-colored neon and mechanical patterns, of gaudy women and sharp-dressed men, reflecting the life of Beale Street in Memphis, where Speller has lived and painted since 1940.

It is a far cry from Speller's rural Mississippi roots. Born into a sharecropping family in Rolling Fork, in the Mississippi Delta, Speller spent his youth and early manhood plowing, planting, and harvesting cotton. Raised mostly by his grandmother, he left home for good at eighteen. When Speller settled in Memphis in 1941, he found work collecting scrap metal, working in the stockyards, and planting trees for the city parks commission, a job he was to hold until he retired in the mid-1960s. Speller had begun to make drawings when he was young, but in Memphis he had the time and, perhaps just as important, the inspiration of a completely new visual environment to begin making art with greater regularity. "The more I draw, the better I be," he once remarked.

Speller draws scenes from his own day-to-day life: cars, houses, public buildings, and the human figure. He works in pencil and crayon on paper. He is well known for his sometimes graphic images of women with exposed breasts and genitalia, including a series of pieces portraying the female singing group The Supremes, with which he has a virtual obsession.

He suffers increasingly from glaucoma and arthritis, and now sketches while sitting in front of the television. Speller was greatly assisted by his second wife, Georgia, until her death in 1987. She encouraged her husband to advertise his work, and he began to display his paintings on the front of their house.

UNTITLED, 1985
Graphite and colored pencil on paper
17½″ × 23½″

UNTITLED, 1986–87
Graphite and colored pencil on paper
16″ × 20″

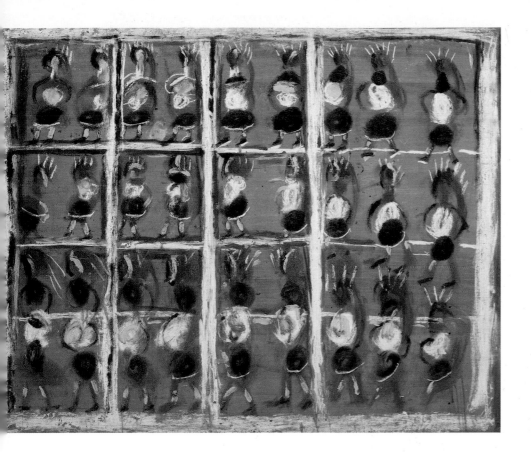

Jimmy Lee Sudduth

(1910–)

Jimmy Sudduth is both a blues musician and a storyteller of considerable energy. He has lived much of his life near Fayette, Alabama, where he worked for many years as a farmhand. He served in the army and married his wife, Ethel, in the 1940s. Sudduth dates the beginnings of his art to his early childhood, and throughout the course of his life he has always managed to find time to make pictures. In his later years, with less to occupy him, Sudduth has become a prolific painter, regularly producing as many as three pictures a day.

Sudduth paints mostly on plywood with a homemade mixture of mud and pigment. He first blocks out the image using what he calls a "dye rock," a soft, porous claylike material that, after being dipped in water, leaves a dark, heavy line when pressed against a hard surface. He then fills in the outline with a mixture of mud and sugar-water. When dried, this "sweet mud" creates a permanent ground onto which he applies color from various fruits, vegetables, and plants. Recently Sudduth began to experiment with coloring his work using house paint brought to him by admirers. Sudduth's subject matter ranges widely, but for the most part he depicts the people and places of Fayette.

WILD INDIANS, 1989
House paint and chalk on plywood
47″ × 54½″

SELF-PORTRAIT WITH CHICKENS, 1988
Paint with mud on wood
31¾″ × 24″

TOTO, 1990
Enamel, mud, and berry juice on plywood
48″ × 24″

UNTITLED, 1988
Paint with mud on wood
15½" × 13"

TOTO, 1988
Paint with mud on wood
31¾″ × 24″

Johnnie Swearingen

(1908–1993)

Powerful though it may be, the Lord's voice sometimes has to repeat itself, according to the Reverend Johnnie Swearingen. The first time the Lord called him to preach, Swearingen has related, he was only seven years old, living near the town of Brenham, Texas. He began to draw at an early age. But a nomadic life that took him to California and back again, a marriage that ended in divorce, and later a career as a farmer in Texas combined to stifle his religious impulses for many years. Swearingen picked cotton and grapes and worked as a longshoreman. By 1948, he had turned his back on at least the practice if not the spirit of religion.

He had not, however, turned his back on art. By the early 1950s, though he was not preaching, he was nevertheless beginning to create the crowded and colorful religious and biblical scenes that eventually made him well known throughout the Southwest. Swearingen paints primarily with oils on Masonite boards, rendering scenes from his past and situations from daily life with humor and imagination. Behind his best works, however, lies the constant awareness of moral responsibility and the certainty of God's judgment. Swearingen began preaching again in 1962 and has continued ever since.

UNTITLED, 1980
Oil on board
16″ × 24″

Mose Tolliver

(1915?–)

While many self-taught artists have dealt with sexual themes indirectly, Mose Tolliver is rare in dealing with them explicitly, even exuberantly. Tolliver's openness to such material may spring in part from an artistic energy that has seen him turn out as many as ten paintings a day.

In the late 1960s, while working in a furniture factory in Georgia, Tolliver suffered an accident in which both his feet were crushed by a falling slab of marble. In the early 1970s, his former employer took him to an art show and suggested that Tolliver take art courses. Tolliver insisted he could do as well without the courses and set to work. He placed his paintings in the yard of his Montgomery, Alabama, house, and when one was sold, he would often duplicate the subject, soon establishing a theme with variations. A few years after he began, his work formed a significant part of the Corcoran Gallery's exhibition "Black Folk Art in America."

Tolliver was one of twelve children raised by a sharecropper family on a farm on Pike Road, outside of Montgomery. His birth date is given as either 1915 or 1919. Tolliver married in the early 1940s and fathered fourteen children. After he moved to Montgomery in the 1940s, he worked as a gardener, truck farmer, and in the shipping department of the furniture company where he was injured. Since then, painting has become the center of Tolliver's life. He works at all hours of the day, painting on plywood, paneling, or Masonite. But he will paint on almost anything his friends bring him, including gourds, beds, chairs, cafeteria trays, and on one occasion even a coffin lid.

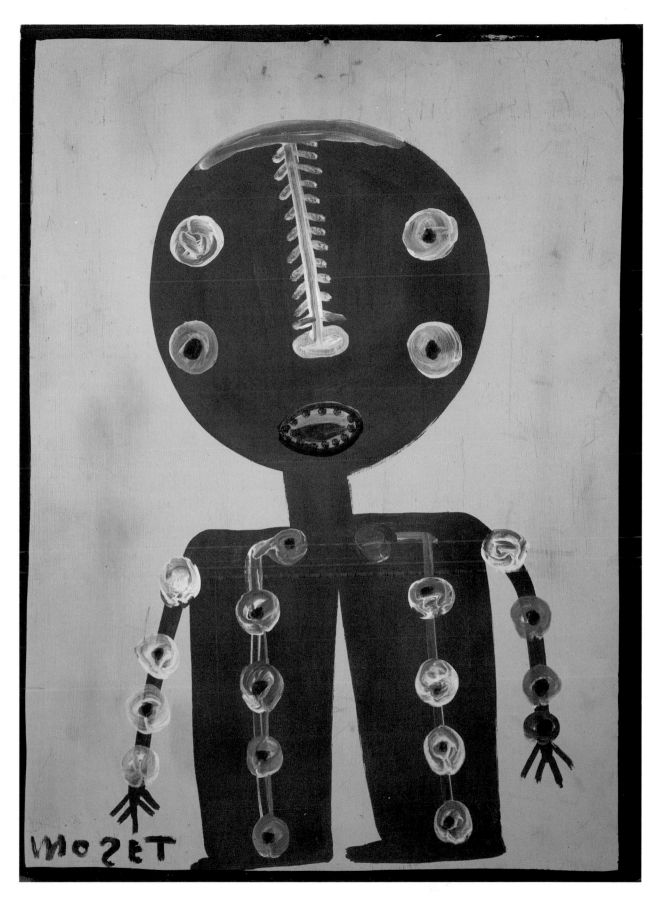

X-RAY MAN, 1985-87
Enamel on wood
23″ × 16¾″

MARTIN LUTHER KING, 1983
Enamel on plywood
20½″ × 24½″

OTIS REDDING, THE DOCK OF THE BAY, 1987–88
Enamel on plywood
23¼″ × 15¾″

UNTITLED, 1985–87
Enamel on wood panel
19½″ × 17⅜″

Bill Traylor

(1854?–1947)

Visitors to the black neighborhood of Montgomery, Alabama, in 1940 would have been treated to an unexpected sight. In front of the Ross-Clayton Funeral Parlor, in a chair next to the Coca-Cola cooler, sat a massive, dignified old man with a board across his lap, drawing. He never stopped. On his small pieces of cardboard sprang to life a world of chicken stealing, hunting, plowing, preaching, drinking, arguing, and testifying, as well as many vivid representations of the animal world. In only three years, between 1939 and 1942, Bill Traylor—former slave, factory worker, and homeless welfare recipient, who slept on a wooden pallet inside the funeral home—created his own extraordinary history of drawing in 1,800 images. Most were preserved by his friend and fellow artist, Charles Shannon. Traylor was black, Shannon white.

Much of what we know about Traylor we owe to Shannon, who provided him with materials and encouragement. Traylor was born a slave on the Traylor plantation near Benton, Alabama, around 1854 and worked there as a field hand until he left for Montgomery. Welfare records indicate that he may have been in Montgomery as early as 1936. He probably began drawing not long before Shannon first saw him. His technique developed rapidly from the use of simple geometric shapes like triangles to complex abstract constructions peopled with multiple tiny figures in motion. Once he began, he worked every day, following the same routine among the jugs of kerosene and sacks of feed his friends had left him to guard, drawing and painting the animals and scenes he remembered from his rural days and the characters in the street around him.

Traylor's work was interrupted in 1942 when he went to stay in several northern cities with his children, none of whom seemed to know what to do with him. During that period he did little, if any, drawing. Upon his return to Montgomery in 1946, he found that everything he knew had changed. He became ill and lost a leg to gangrene. The social agency that supplied his welfare check discovered a daughter living in Montgomery and insisted he live with her. Unhappy in his new situation, Traylor lost the desire to work. He died in a nursing home, a few days after summoning Charles Shannon for a final visit.

Shannon arranged for a showing of Traylor's work in Montgomery and in 1941 had his drawings taken to the Museum of Modern Art. After Traylor's death, Shannon began a prolonged effort to bring that work to the public. Today Traylor's work is regarded as among the major triumphs of self-taught art.

ONE LEGGED MAN, 1939–42
Compressed charcoal on paper
15½″ × 9⅜″

RED HOUSE WITH FIGURES, 1939–42
Pencil, poster paint, and crayon on cardboard
22″ × 14″

FIGURE WITH CONSTRUCTION ON BACK, 1940
Pencil and poster paint on cardboard
12⅜″ × 8¼″

MAN RIDING A BIRD, 1939–42
Tempera on cardboard
17″ × 11″

TWO FIGHTING DOGS, 1939–42
Pencil and poster paint on cardboard
27½″ × 22¼″

FIGURE CONSTRUCTION, 1939–42
Tempera and pencil on cardboard
14″ × 9″

Gegorio Valdes
(1879–1939)

In front of the shop of Gregorio Valdes in Key West, Florida, hung a palette-shaped sign lettered with the words G. VALDES SIGN PAINTER. In addition to that work, however, Valdes often painted on commission for members of Key West's literary and artistic community. He painted the house where poet Elizabeth Bishop stayed in the town; among his patrons were Edwin Denby and Rudolph Burkhardt. Orson Welles owned one of his pictures.

Bishop described the first painting of Valdes she saw: "The sky was blue at the top, then white, then beautiful blush pink, the pink of a hot, mosquito-filled tropical evening." She bought the painting, for three dollars.

Valdes's career recalls an earlier time, when art was also the trade of a multitude of itinerant craftsmen who, for a price, would memorialize people and places in lieu of (and prior to the advent of) photographs. Valdes was born in Key West and lived most of his life there. Painting was his primary trade, and with it he supported his Cuban-born wife and a family of five daughters and two sons.

Around the corner from his residence Valdes rented a decaying house as his studio. He accepted commissions from locals and visitors and also advertised that he did paintings by mail order. People desiring something more substantial than a mere photograph would send snapshots or postcards and money, and Valdes would send back the painted "copy," usually far different in effect. One of the people who sent an image to Valdes was the art dealer Sidney Janis, whose choice was a bouquet of roses. Janis received a card a few weeks later saying that Valdes had fallen ill and, soon thereafter, a second note, from Valdes's daughter, saying that the artist had died before he could complete Janis's commission. Janis included him in his landmark 1942 book, *They Taught Themselves: American Primitive Painters of the Twentieth Century.*

Valdes prided himself on his realism and boasted that he once deceived his uncle with a picture of a towel rack and a towel, which he hung up over the wash basin in place of the real thing. His "method" was at the same time a limitation and the source of his visual power. He flattened, reduced, simplified, and schematized photographs. But what was lost in detail, he gained in atmosphere and a kind of architectural stateliness.

UNTITLED, 1938–40
Oil on canvas
25″ × 35½″

Gregory Van Maanen

(1947–)

Before Gregory Van Maanen was wounded in combat in Vietnam in 1969—on a patrol he calls his "night of white light"—he was a patriotic draftee from an ordinary American background. Afterward, everything, including his spiritual condition, was changed. The impulse to make art was the final confirmation of a radical break with the past.

Van Maanen was born in Paterson, New Jersey, to a working-class family. He was drafted into the army out of high school in 1968. He spent nine months in Okinawa and Korea recovering from his injuries before returning to the United States a committed pacifist. He began to paint and sculpt in 1971, attended Ramapo College in 1972, and began to travel, particularly to Mexico.

Van Maanen's painting was at first based on abstract forms of what appeared to be alien, almost extraterrestrial, organic entities. But gradually the development of his work showed these shapes becoming the basis for a personal and powerful visual vocabulary. In paintings done in the 1980s, Van Maanen moved toward Mexican and Latin American motifs, perhaps less the result of conscious borrowing than of archetypal convergence. Van Maanen uses his work as a psychic daybook, jotting notes, dates, and symbols on the back of each canvas. These recall both events and states of mind that either influenced the painting or were evoked by it during and after its creation.

UNTITLED, 1989
Acrylic and enamel on board
16¼" × 15¾"

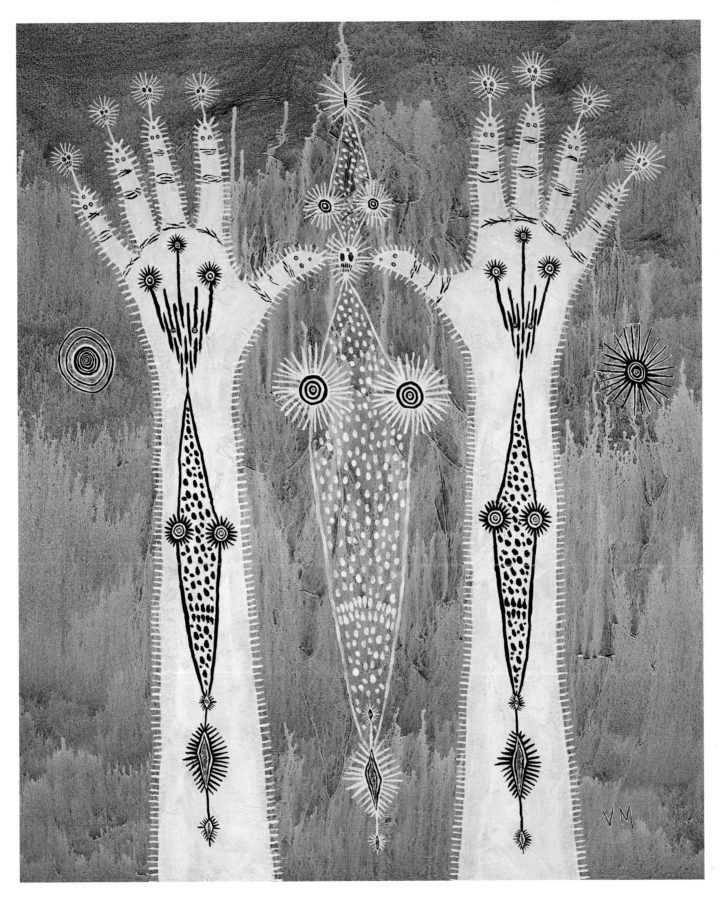

UNTITLED, 1989
Acrylic and enamel on board
30¼″ × 24¼″

Gregory Van Maanen / 255

Eugene Von Bruenchenhein

(1910–1983)

Early in 1954, news of nuclear testing awakened in Eugene Von Bruenchenhein, who was then employed in a Milwaukee bakery, an overwhelming awareness of the potential for a holocaust. This vision of destruction demanded tools of expression only painting could provide, and for most of the next three decades Von Bruenchenhein detailed a vast and luminous imaginative universe, one that included such creatures as might appear under a microscope along with cataclysmic events in the cosmos. Manipulating the paint with his fingers, with brushes he made from his wife's hair, and with other objects, Von Bruenchenhein created a pulsating, organic art.

Then, he suddenly stopped painting for more than a decade in the mid-1960s. When he resumed, it was to detail a different but equally ambitious architectural vision. In a poem titled "The Universe Unlimited," Von Bruenchenhein wrote: "Test me—I have gone out to / a colorful universe— / . . . of beauty—unknown to man / and vision and imagination . . ."

Von Bruenchenhein's paintings were part of a monumental artistic output that included sculptures made of chicken bones, masks made of concrete, poetry, prose, and thousands of experimental photographs, most of them erotic, made in collaboration with his wife, Marie, whom he married in 1943. This trove, discovered in the artist's modest Milwaukee home after his death, had its origins as early as 1930, when Von Bruenchenhein began to write poetry. He also pursued an interest in horticulture and worked for a florist for a time. He drew heavily on images from this experience in his later paintings.

After Von Bruenchenhein's death, friends concerned about his wife's finances contacted the Kohler Arts Center to see if his work had value. The first exhibition of his work was mounted there a few months after his death.

UNTITLED, 1957
Oil on board
24″ × 24″

UNTITLED, 1957
Oil on board
24″ × 24″

Inez Nathaniel Walker

(1911–1990)

Inez Walker was born in Sumter, South Carolina. Like Nellie Mae Rowe, Walker decided in her twenties that farm life was too rigorous— "The muck would eat you up," she once remarked. By that time both her parents were dead. She was already married and had four children. She moved north with them around 1930 to Philadelphia, where she worked in a pickle plant. She lost her job during a strike in 1949 and moved to Port Byron, New York, where she worked on apple farms.

For Walker, the door to art was opened by tragedy. In 1970 she was convicted of criminally negligent homicide in the killing of a man who had apparently abused her, and she was sent to the Bedford Hills Correctional Facility. She began to draw—at first on the backs of sheets of the prison newspaper—as a way, she says, of isolating and protecting herself from the "bad girls" around her. Perhaps as a result, her art, consisting primarily of portraits of women done in pencil, ink, crayon, felt marker, and watercolor, gives the sense of being wholly self-generated. The patterned details of clothing and backgrounds seem a direct reaction to her prison environment, an expression of her experience with the prison's surrounding order.

Walker insisted that she never worked from models, though many of the drawings, in which the eyes are the focus, bear a striking resemblance to the artist. A prison English teacher took an interest in her work and showed it to a gallery owner in Bedford Hills, where Walker was given her first show in 1972. The same year, she was released from prison and moved back to upstate New York. There, while working as a seasonal farm laborer, she married again. Later separated from her husband, in 1980 she disappeared from view and after 1986 was intermittently a patient at the Willard Psychiatric Center in upstate New York. She worked only sporadically until her death from pancreatic cancer.

UNTITLED, 1977
Graphite, colored pencil, and pen on paper
18″ × 11¾″

Perley Meyer ("P. M.") Wentworth

(ACTIVE CA. 1950–1960)

At an exhibition of self-taught art in the mid-1950s, a man introduced himself to Dr. Tarmo Pasto, the psychologist who discovered the work of Martín Ramírez (page 185) and other self-taught artists, and offered to show him a cache of drawings. They were the work of P. M. Wentworth, who left behind some forty drawings. The little that is known of Wentworth himself has come through the references in and inscriptions on those drawings. It has been established that Wentworth, who died around 1960, was active in both southern California and the San Francisco Bay area, where he worked as a night watchman, during the 1950s. This may well have been his most active period, though some of his pictures have been dated as early as the 1930s.

Wentworth presents visions of landscapes and architectures that seem at once prehistoric and extraterrestrial. Many of his references are biblical, and his topography and the contours of his stone structures and landscapes are fluid and organic. Wentworth indicated that his visions came from gazing at the night sky and could be duplicated by confronting the blankness of a sheet of paper. He used pencil to give his elements a clear outline, then added gouache and crayon, which he assiduously rubbed into the paper to give his colors an almost translucent quality. In the final stage he went over his drawings with an eraser. Perhaps to maintain the basic distinction between inner life and outer world, perhaps to reiterate the primary faculty of apprehension and creation, Wentworth at some point began to label his drawings with the word "imagination."

UNTITLED, 1955
Pencil, tempera, and crayon on paper
30″ × 25½″

UNTITLED, 1940
Pencil, crayon, and gouache on paper
25½″ × 30″

Luster Willis

(1913–)

The area around Crystal Springs, Mississippi, was a fertile ground for early blues music. It was also home to two important self-taught artists, who never met one another: O. W. Kitchens (page 117) and the sculptor and painter Luster Willis, whose work is rooted in the blues.

"This Is It!" proclaims one of Willis's favorite inscriptions, which usually accompanies the image of a person staring amazedly at an enormous fish. This exclamatory quality, combining spectacle, allegory, and exhortation, runs through many of Willis's paintings, from his skeletal mummies made ghostlike by applied glitter to his depictions of such recurrent rural routines as a hog killing. Every image seems to harbor a larger moral significance, to offer a lesson, just as blues songs draw larger patterns from the stories they tell.

Willis, who was born near Terry, Mississippi, has often remarked that he is inspired to paint a picture when he feels lonely or blue. He was born into a family of blues musicians, but was himself attracted more to art than to music. As a child, he drew constantly, especially in the classroom, where his efforts incurred only the wrath of teachers. After he left school, Willis worked variously as a barber, farm worker, and woodcutter in and around Crystal Springs, leaving the area only to serve in the military in France, Germany, and Austria from 1943 to 1947.

Willis structures many of his images around an almost geometrical sense of perspective. In others, his trademark use of glitter emphasizes surface over illusionistic depth. In addition to such materials as glitter and shoe polish, Willis has used silhouetting, collage, and tempera and watercolor textures. A stroke in 1986 has left him partially paralyzed and unable to work consistently. As with a number of important self-taught artists, Willis first gained major recognition for his art after the Corcoran Gallery's 1982 "Black Folk Art in America" exhibition.

THIS IS IT. THE BIG ONE, 1979–80
Tempera and glitter on paper
18″ × 27¼″

SELF PORTRAIT WITH UNDERTAKER FRIEND, 1947
Tempera, shoe polish, and paint on paper
10½″ × 16″

Joseph Elmer Yoakum

(1886–1972)

Only a handful of American self-taught artists have devoted themselves exclusively to landscapes. By far the most prodigious, in terms of both output and ambition, is Joseph Yoakum. His several thousand drawings, produced over a decade, document an entire globe of locations, from *Mt. Golleia on North Portion of Antarctica In So West Pacific Ocean* to *Mt. Demaveno near Meshad, Iran.* These forms are composed of strong convoluted and undulating lines done in felt-tipped or ballpoint pens, usually, though not always, filled in with pastels and watercolors. Yoakum often worked with tracing paper, using earlier drawings to provide a "patron," as he called it. He claimed to have seen firsthand nearly all the locations he depicted, but the drawings themselves are less about the particular look of a place than about the manifold forms of a tremendous and sustaining natural energy.

Yoakum was attracted to the exotic, even legendary, quality of the places he drew. He owned an atlas and other geographical reference works, and he used the place names as inspiration for a vast visual fiction. Likewise, his autobiography gives the sense of an ambitious imaginative enterprise. Yoakum claims to have been born a Navajo on the reservation at Window Rock, near Winslow, Arizona. After moving to Missouri, he ran away from home in his early teens to join the circus, traveling the country as a roustabout for such well-known shows of the day as the Adams Forbaugh, the Buffalo Bill, and the Ringling circuses. He claimed to have been personal valet to circus magnate John Ringling. Yoakum continued wandering as a railroad porter, hobo, and stowaway. He asserted he had visited every continent except Antarctica before he went to France with the army in World War I. He married twice and fathered five children.

In 1962, at age seventy-six, living alone in a public housing project in Chicago, Yoakum was inspired by a dream to begin drawing. He began to render the geography of the globe in colored pencil and ballpoint through a process he called "spiritual unfoldment." His landscapes are animate and at times transparent—critic John Ollman has described the images as "X-rays" of the scenes whose locations Yoakum inscribed in their margins.

A storyteller with a powerful presence, Yoakum attracted both customers and admirers. Working in what had been an old barbershop on the South Side of Chicago, Yoakum hung his work for sale in the window as he finished it. He became famous locally—his work was championed by Chicago artists including

Jim Nutt—and the subject of serious critical attention and exhibitions, first by the Chicago Museum of Contemporary Art and later by the Museum of Modern Art. But he never sought attention and was suspicious of it when it was given. He worked, often turning out a drawing a day, until he died in a Chicago hospital on Christmas in 1972.

JUDEAN HILLS NEAR DEAD SEA, 1966
Colored pencil on brown paper
12″ × 18″

MT. SHASTA OF COAST RANGE, 1964–68
Colored pencil, watercolor, and pen on paper
11⅞″ × 18⅞″

MT. BALDY IN BEAVER HEAD RANGE NEAR HUMPHERY, ID, 12/27/69
Colored pencil and pen on paper
12″ × 19″

VIEW OF THE ARCTIC OCEAN AT SYDNEY, AUSTRALIA, 1970
Colored pencil and pen on paper
12″ × 18″

SAC RIVER—ASH GROVE, MONTANA, 1960
Colored pencil, watercolor, and pen on paper
9" × 12"

MOUNT TENGRIKHAN, 10/22/69
Colored pencil with watercolor on paper
19″ × 12″

Purvis Young

(1943–)

In 1973 residents of Miami first became aware of Purvis Young's art through a highly visible, even provocative, display. Over a two-year period Young attached hundreds of his paintings to the wall of a dilapidated building north of downtown. In this vast project—Goodbread Alley—Young managed to capture the haste, energy, and struggle of Overtown, the African-American neighborhood where he was born and grew up. A decade later Young attempted works of similar scope, but this time in an official capacity: he was commissioned to decorate first the auditorium of the Miami Dade Public Library, then the exterior of the Culmer Overtown Branch Library, where for years Young had been a frequent visitor, studying art in the books he found there.

Convicted and sentenced in the late 1960s for armed robbery, Young was encouraged to draw by a sympathetic prison attendant. In the mid-1970s, Young, who had been storing drawings inside discarded books, began to illustrate and alter those books, producing a powerful complement to his drawings. In one of those books he wrote, "The street is life." The streets of Miami eventually came to provide not only his subjects, but also his material—plywood, plaster, nails, glass, plastic. Young's swift, gestural style, which is capable of both delicacy and bluntness, suits his role as unofficial historian of Overtown and chronicler of the lives of its citizens. His images, which may contain dream animals, quasi-allegorical personages, or local characters, veer from celebration to anger as they attempt to express the reality of economic disadvantage. Young feels strong artistic kinship with the Abstract Expressionists, whose work he has admired in books. He has transformed his experience of the street not only into social commentary but into personal mythology.

HORSES, 1987–88
Enamel on wood
40½″ × 48¼″

UNTITLED, 1980–82
Enamel on board
48″ × 58″

AGAIN, 1987–88
Tempera on board
44¼″ × 26¼″

Unknown Artists

BOTANICAL GARDENS, 1946
Charcoal pencil and oil on canvas
19¾″ × 25⅜″

UNTITLED, 1955
Enamel on board
29⅝″ × 24½″

UNTITLED, 1920–30
Oil on canvas
29½" × 24¼"

UNTITLED, 1950–55
Fabric dye on cotton sheet
46″ × 64″

ALL WE ASK IS A FAIR TRIAL, 1920–30
Oil on canvas
36″ × 46″

UNTITLED, 1920–30
Oil on canvas
15½″ × 15½″

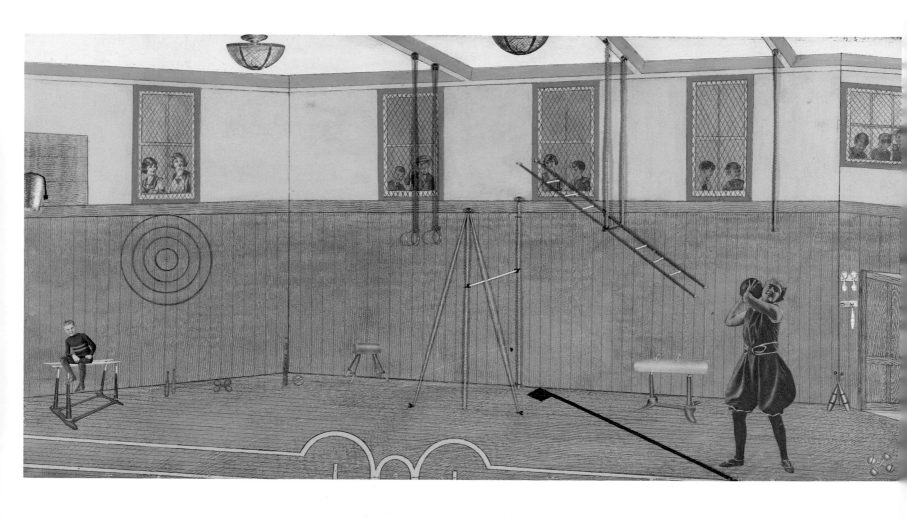

GYM SCENE, 1930
Mixed media on academy board
21″ × 40½″

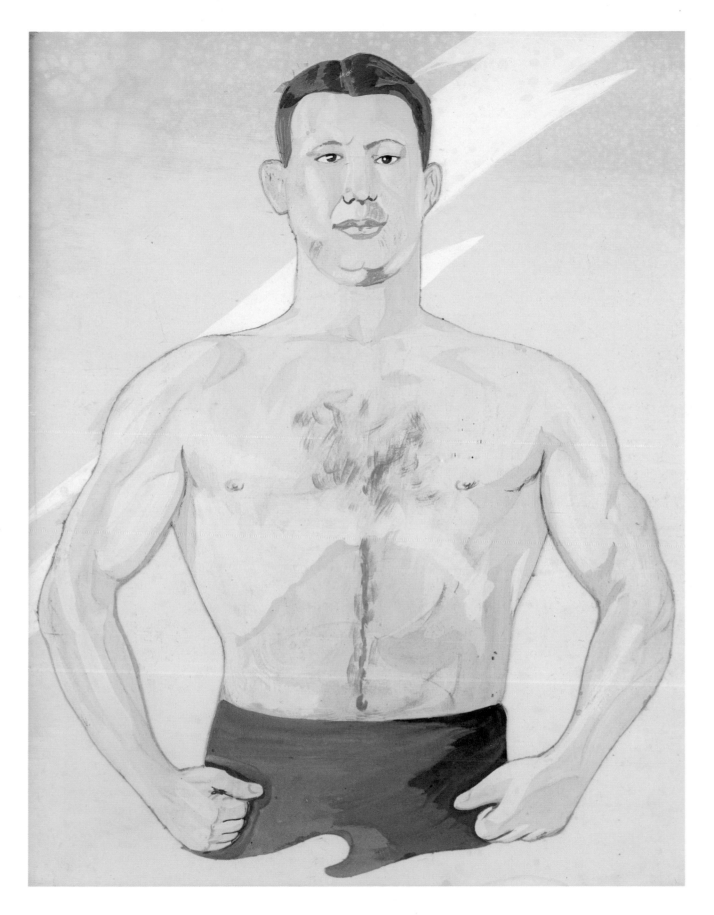

UNTITLED, 1915—20
Tempera on cardboard
22″ × 17½″

COLONEL LINDBERG, signed Faust, 1976
Oil on canvas
30″ × 40″

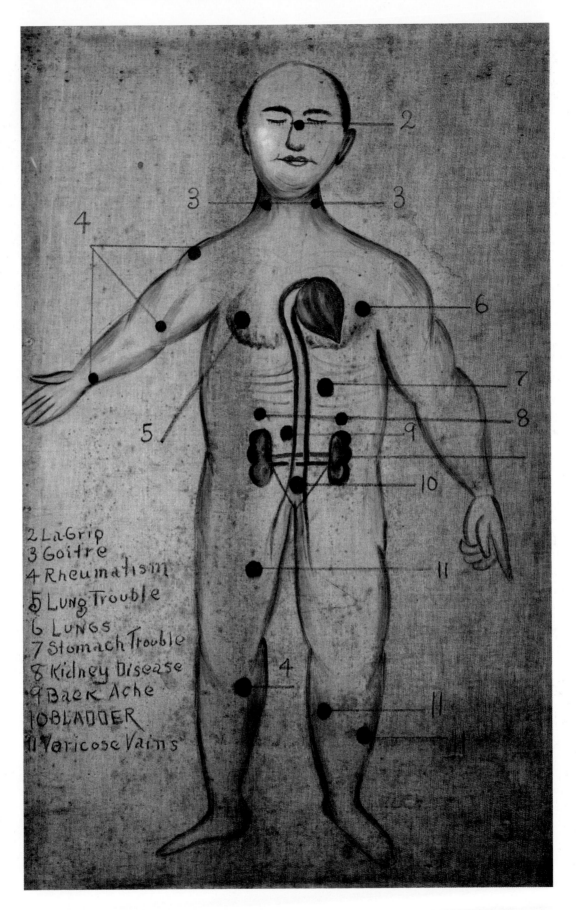

UNTITLED, 1930–40
Gouache on linen
44¼″ × 27″

UNTITLED, 1900—15
Enamel on paper
22¾″ × 26¼″

UNTITLED, signed Kelly, 1950–55
Oil on canvas
16″ × 12″

UNTITLED (TRADE DINER SIGN), CA 1940–50
Enamel on plywood
36″ × 30″

UNTITLED, 1900–15
Oil on canvas
22¾" × 26¼"

UNTITLED, 1931
Oil over relief wood carving
17¼″ × 27⅝″

FAT LADY, 1930–40
Oil on canvas
39″ × 70″

page 4 "Every style": John Berger, "The Cherished and the Excluded," introduction to *Prison Paintings* by Michael Quanne (London: John Murray, 1985), 2–3.

9 "That's hard work": Alexander Sackton, "Eddie Arning: The Man," exhibition catalogue, (Williamsburg, Va.: Abby Aldrich Rockefeller Folk Art Center, 1985), 11.

28 "a celebration": Mary Elaine Lora, "The Tin Man," *Louisiana Life,* vol. 2, no. 2 (1982), 109.

35 "picked up a piece": Susan Chadwick, "Con Artist—Prison Unlocks Wealth of Talent in Convict," *Houston Post,* December 13, 1989, C4.

"the almighty buck": Statement by the artist, 1989.

"I didn't know": Chadwick, "Con Artist," C4.

"They can lock": Statement by the artist, 1989.

53 "Art ain't about": Interview with Thornton Dial, Sr., by Paul and William Arnett, 1990.

"recycle": Ibid

63 "If you like": Interview with Butler and Lisa Hancock, by Frank Maresca and Roger Ricco, January 1991.

67 "You know": Kay Sloman, "Antonio Esteves: Brooklyn Folk Painter," unpublished article (1982), 4.

78 "I was always": Gene Epstein, "The Art and Times of Victor Joseph Gatto," in *The Clarion,* the magazine of the Museum of American Folk Art, vol. 13, no. 2 (1988), 57.

80 Material for this essay is taken in part from the following: Chuck and Jan Rosenak, *Museum of American Folk Art Encyclopedia of Twentieth Century American Folk Art and Artists* (New York: Abbeville Press, 1990), 139–41; Chuck Rosenak, "Artist and Daughter Re-united," *The Clarion,* magazine of the Museum of American Folk Art, vol. 16, no. 2 (1991), 16; interviews with Lee Godie by Russell Bowman and Carl Hammer.

84 "The more I": "Another Face of the Diamond: Pathways through the Black Atlantic South," exhibition catalogue (New York: INTAR Latin American Gallery, 1988), 63.

89 "You have to": Gary Schwindler and William L. Hawkins, "William L. Hawkins," exhibition catalogue (New York: Ricco/Maresca Gallery, August 1990), 3.

112 "The city is": Sidney Janis, *They Taught Themselves: American Primitive Painters of the Twentieth Century* (New York: Dial Press, 1942), 77.

"to hire himself": Ibid.

117 "Of course I": "Some excerpts from the lifes [sic] history of O. W. 'Pappy' Kitchens," written statement by the artist, early 1980s, supplied by William Dunlap.

120 "gorgeous and colorful festivities": Statement by the artist, late 1960s.

124 "But I had": Written statement by the artist for Wisconsin State Fair Festival of Arts, June 1965.

126 "It's not about": Eleanor Gaver, "Inside the Outsiders," *Art and Antiques,* vol. 7, no. 6 (1990), 81.

130 "a regular necessity": Interview with Annie Lucas by Marcia Weber, August 1990.

136 "miracle pieces": Interview with Bonnie Grossman, artist's agent, by Lyle Rexer, September 1990.

150 "thrown out on": Rosenak, *American Folk Art Encyclopedia,* 369.

155 "Satan is always": John Beardsley and Jane Livingston, *Black Folk Art in America,* 1930–1980 (Jackson, Miss.: University Press of Mississippi, 1982), 101.

159 "I try to": Interview with Lenny Kesl, artist's friend, by Lyle Rexer, December 1990.

161 "When I started": Statement by the artist, *Another Face of the Diamond: Pathways through the Black Atlantic South,* exhibition catalogue (New York: INTAR Latin American Gallery, 1988), 65.

173 "to keep from": Kathy Kemp, "His Work Is God and Gourds," *Kudzu* magazine, Birmingham *Post-Herald,* July 10, 1987.

175 "Every piece of wood": John Beardsley and Jane Livingston, *Black Folk Art in America,* 1930⁻1980 (Jackson, Miss.: University Press of Mississippi, 1982), 120.

179 "My opinion of art": Holger Cahill et al., *Masters of Popular Painting: Modern Primitives of Europe and America,* exhibition catalogue (New York: Museum of Modern Art, 1938), 126.

185 "He is neither": Octavio Paz, "Art and Identity: Hispanics in the United States," in John Beardsley and Jane Livingston, *Hispanic Art in the United States* (New York: Abbeville Press, 1987), 28.

193 "in an unbelievably": Excerpts from the artist's notebooks, provided by Bonnie Grossman, artist's agent.

199 "Drawing is the only": Interview with Nellie Mae Rowe by Judith Alexander, 1982.

211 "The most difficult": Kristine McKenna, "Inside the Mind of an Artistic Outsider," *Los Angeles Times/Calender,* November 12, 1989.

215 "only pure, realistic paintings": Interview with Drossos Skyllas by Phyllis Kind, artist's agent, 1971.

228 "I feel like": Interview with Simon Sparrow by René Paul Barilleux, *Art Muscle,* vol. 2, no. 5 (1988), 15, 17.

254 "night of white light": Interview with Randall Morris, artist's agent, by Lyle Rexer, August 1990.

256 "Test me—": "Eugene Von Bruenchenhein: Wisconsin Visionary," exhibition announcement (Sheboygan, Wis.: John Michael Kohler Arts Center, 1984), 5.

259 "The muck would": "Self-Taught Artist Discovered in Prison," *Correctional Services News,* vol. 3, no. 6 (1978), 5.

"Those are eagle": Interview with Willie White by Richard Gasperi, mid-1980s.

266 "patron": John Ollman, foreword in *Animistic Landscapes: Joseph Yoakum Drawings,* exhibition catalogue (Philadelphia: Janet Fleisher Gallery, 1989), 10.

"spiritual unfoldment": Interview with Joseph Yoakum by Jim Nutt, ca. 1970.

Photographic Permissions

Judith Alexander: 85, 200, 201 (bottom), 202

Amenoff/Faust: 255

Ames Gallery of American Folk Art: 137, 194, 195, 196

Aarne Anton: 243

William Arnett: 53, 54, 129 (top), 126, 127, 222, 225, 232

John and Diane Balsley: 23 (bottom), 51, 125

David and Didi Barrett: 214

Deborah Barrett: 212

Estate of Dr. Robert Bishop: 18, 68, 209

Bob Blumert and Jackie Fiore: 74 (bottom), 118 (top), 130, 144, 183, 205, 272, 287

Barbara and Russell Bowman: 80, 81

Norman Brosterman: 279

Irene Ward Brydon: 135 (top)

Janice and Mickey Cartin: 113, 114, 219

Cavin-Morris Gallery: 108 (top), 110, 153, 203, 207, 213

Allan Daniel: 293

David Davies: 65, 66, 138 (bottom), 138 (top), 190

Epstein/Powell Gallery: 79

William Fagaly: 118 (bottom), 142, 163

Janet Fleisher Gallery: 176, 177, 181

Richard Gasperi: 29, 30 (top), 30 (bottom), 31, 104 (top), 104

(bottom), 105, 119, 265

Marcy and Elias Getz: 14, 15, 145, 210, 286

Kurt Gitter and Alice Rae Yellen: 155, 157, 158, 160, 162, 173, 223

Robert M. Greenberg: 42–3, 55 (top), 73, 74 (top), 94, 186, 217, 224, 227, 236, 241

Creative Growth Arts Center: 134 (top), 134 (bottom), 135 (bottom)

Carl Hammer Gallery: 48, 230, 257

Butler and Lisa Hancock: 63, 64

Herbert Waide Hemphill: 120, 139, 184, 198, 249, 254

Hill Gallery: 284

Timothy and Pamela Hill: 13 (bottom)

Hillman Gemini Gallery: 111, 191, 192

Estate of Morris Hirshfield: 97

Purchased with funds from Mrs. L. Hopkins: 251

Sidney Janis Gallery: 98, 99, 100

Art Jones: 115, 116

Elyse Kaftan and Patrice Pluto: 250

Timothy Keny: 172

Phyllis Kind Gallery: 19 (bottom), 21, 38, 39, 76, 187, 189, 215, 216

Amanda Knight: 49

Louanne La Roche: 60, 61, 234, 237

Frank Maresca: 32, 33 (top), 33 (bottom), 34, 46–7, 58, 93, 141, 149 (bottom), 164, 281, 285, 290, 292

Marvill Collection: 56, 90, 276, 288, 291

Donald McKenny: 44–5 (bottom)

Michael and Gael Mendelsohn: 11 (bottom), 75, 121, 149 (top), 244

Menil Collection: 37 (bottom)

Barnaby Millard: 52

Milwaukee Art Museum—Hall Collection: 218

Randall and Sherri Morris and John and Anne Ollman: 182

Museum of American Folk Art—Gift of Elizabeth Ross Johnson: 77, 165

Museum of American Folk Art—Gift of Shirley Paris: 278

Museum of American Folk Art—Gift of Charles B. Rosenak: 102

Jim Nutt and Gladys Nilsson: 185, 188, 262

Richard H. Oosterom: 156

Christoper N. B. Owles: 83

Martin and Enid Packard: 178

Private Collection: 28, 40–1, 44–5(top), 51, 91, 92, 103, 106, 107, 108 (bottom), 129 (bottom), 131, 132, 180, 199, 201 (top), 208, 269, 270, 271, 275, 280

Robert Reeves: 159

Siri Von Reis: 204, 246, 264, 267, 268

Roger Ricco: 10, 26 (bottom), 95, 146, 147

Ricco/Johnson Gallery: 229

Ricco/Maresca Gallery: 11 (top), 12, 13 (top), 19 (top), 82, 84, 86, 87 (top), 87 (bottom), 123, 166, 167, 168, 169, 174, 221, 231, 253, 274, 283, 289

Lois and Richard Rosenthal: 282

Luise Ross Gallery: 70

Andrew and Linda Safran: 233

Judy Saslow: 247, 248

Kerry Schuss: 27

The Shelp Collection: 55 (bottom), 128

Murray Smither: 109

William Steen: 36, 37 (top)

Dr. Nancy F. Karlins Thoman: 154, 260

Edward Thorp Gallery: 258

Spencer Throckmorton: 239

Clune Walsh: 171

Lanford Wilson: 16, 20, 25, 26 (top), 59, 62, 67, 69, 71, 78, 88, 143, 235, 242, 263

Mr. and Mrs. Charles Zadok: 151

A Note on the Type

The text of this book was set in a digitized version of Fournier, a typeface originated by Pierre Simon Fournier *fils* (1712–1768). Coming
from a family of typefounders, Fournier was an extraordinarily
prolific designer both of typefaces and of typographic ornaments.
He was also the author of the celebrated *Manuel typographique*
(1764–1766). In addition, he was the first to attempt to work
out the point system standardizing type measurement
that is still in use internationally.
The cut of the typeface named for this remarkable man
captures many of the aspects of his personality and period.
Though it is elegant, it is also very legible.

Composed by Sarabande Press,
New York, New York

Printed and bound by Dai Nippon Printing,
Hong Kong

Designed by Iris Weinstein